sam parish

COOK ME*
*please

30 dishes/3 ways, 90 lip-smacking recipes!

KOA PRESS

photography by tonia shuttleworth

CON-
TENTS

I'm so glad you decided to COOK ME. I know it takes a lot to get into cook mode – I'm talking full-blown, recipe-out, ingredients-bought, apron-on, ready-to-get-amongst-the-rhythm-of-the-kitchen mode. I totally get it. But it is my hope that with this book you will be inspired to get in there and well . . . cook. Yes, this is your recipe book talking (but also the author), and I'm asking you to please cook my pages, cover me in food (less the author here) and reap the rewards of recipes inspired and written with maximum of flavour and minimum of fuss (thank you, Antonio Carluccio and Gennaro Contaldo*) in mind.

These over-confident recipes are here to restore your faith in cooking at home, by making it an exciting act you can be a part of three times a day if you like. (That's slightly ambitious I know, but who wants to be hangry?)

You will hear from me throughout these pages, in the hope that I steady you and set a casualness of sorts to grant you confidence in your kitchen. I believe so much in you as the cook and in my recipes, but it's important to remember: this isn't rocket science, and we should truly enjoy the ride.

These recipes are yum, worth-it and achievable. I spend a lot of my day thinking about the next meal and what I can be doing now to make it the best. Whether it's throwing some onions in a bowl with some vinegar to pickle, getting a dough together to prove slowly in the corner or marinating some thick chunks of meat so they have an extra layer of flavour, I'm never not striving for my food to always be MAXIMUM of flavour. And by making these small steps in advance, in turn, minimal fuss. And yes, sometimes that does require more than one spice or more than one type of onion. But trust the process – it's all for flavour, and I wouldn't put it in there if I didn't see its value to the recipe.

I hope this book teaches you these small tricks for how to cook smart and not hard. Because at the end of the day cooking is the most human thing you can do. I mean I might be wrong, but I don't see any other creature doing it. So get in there and COOK ME!

Lè go.

Sam Parish

---

*A note on 'MOFMOF': Maximum of flavour, minimum of fuss – it's a phrase that inspired me very early in my career. Coined by the beautiful Antonio Carluccio and Gennaro Contaldo, it spoke to me, and it became something of a mission for me to spread the ethos. To me it is about cooking smarter not harder, fuss-free and simple, but not basic in flavour. I'd like to take a moment to extend a big thank you to the incredible Contaldo and the late great Carluccio for sharing this message of cooking. It's a type of cooking I think we can all get behind.

A BIT ABOUT ME...

With over ten years' experience in food writing and hospo, I've made a profession in cooking for both media and restaurant dining settings. I was crazy enough to train as a chef while also studying an undergrad bachelor's degree in media, writing and anthropology. In my time I have worked as a chef, consultant, recipe developer, food editor, writer, food stylist, podcaster and TV and video producer. I have worked as a chef all over Australia, even working at the Google Australia restaurant before making the cross into food media. This experience in the kitchen and on the pass makes me the chef and cook I am today.

I can also thank my time on the pans for my understanding of food from different cultures, a testament to the multitude of chefs I've had the privilege of working alongside – in this profession it's the ability to share knowledge that sets a chef apart from the rest and I've been blessed with some incredible teachers. For anyone out there thinking about becoming a chef, it truly opens up a whole world of possibilities!

I got my start in publishing working at the *Australian Women's Weekly* test kitchens, then moved on to *Donna Hay*, where I got to work on my first cookbook. From there I applied and got a position on the food team for *delicious* magazine Australia, and worked my way up to assistant food editor. It was here on this incredibly skilled and experienced small team I had opportunities to travel and learn from some of the best in food media, and to craft my skills in all things food editing, styling and writing.

Since leaving that role I've worked for myself in a freelance capacity. I've worked as a food producer on TV shows, travelled overseas for food festivals, assisted on TV segments, written recipes for publications, food-styled and directed videos, starred in how-to videos, started my own podcast and worked on cookbooks for other amazing foodies.

I'm known for recipes that work, that are complex in flavour and simple in execution. It all comes back to this.

REAI

HOW IT ALL WORKS

O M E *

*please

This is the bit of the book
I know you're tempted to flip
past and pretend doesn't
exist. But come on, at least
give it a skim read. This is not
a drill – turn the page, read
me, then COOK ME, then eat
the yummy things . . .

GOOD THINGS COME IN THREES*

I'm sure you're hankering for someone to *please explain* the 3-way scenario of these recipes. Well, I'm glad you asked. This is a cookbook with the freedom to choose: 30 dishes cooked 3 ways, giving you 90 lip-smacking recipes with maximum flavour and minimum fuss. For each dish we have 3 versions . . .

*I am the third child afterall

01
SLAP IT TOGETHER

These are my 'hack-style' recipes that are even more minimum fuss than usual. This one's all about putting convenience and flavour first and getting you a result with the smallest effort required. Cooking smart not hard and reaping the rewards in mouthfuls of deliciousness. A quick game's a good game, right?

02
GO TO

These are my ride-or-die, tried-and-true recipes that are on heavy rotation at my place and will never go out of style. From fish burgers, to egg and shrooms on doorstop toast to flexi vegan banana bread (yes, totes a thing) they've been developed by me over the years to be the best of the best. The first recipe I reach for when cooking the chosen dish, these are the recipes that make me COOK and I hope inspire you to as well.

03
LONG GAME

These are my not-so-fast, not-so-casual recipes. Sometimes we do have a bit more time up our sleeves and want to go the full nine yards. These recipes have elements that require a little more effort but are worth it for the result – and fear not! They still have a minimum of fuss approach to see us learning something new but not being chained to the stove for seven hours. Cos let's be honest, who's got time for that?

EASY PEASY ICONS

These recipes are loaded with tips and tricks. So to make life EVEN easier, and so you get the job done and find your way asap, there are some fun icons to guide you through . . .

veg/vegan
I've popped this sticker on the recipes that are veg or vegan but there are plenty more that can easily be adapted to be veg or vegan. And FYI, there's an icon down the bottom of the page for those.

makes/serves
Serves usually sit around 4, with the odd recipe serving 1–2 and the bigger share-style recipes 6–8. As for sweets, well, I had to write 12 for some but I totally understand if you bake the carrot cake on page 292 and it serves 1 . . .

prep/cook
These are the bane of my existence. Cos really who knows how long it takes you to cut an onion, and there's no judgement with this – take your time. Think of them as a guide but you do you – you always do you.

begin recipe 1 day ahead
You'll see this icon on recipes when they need you to get acquainted prior to the partayyy. Trust the process, some recipes just need that little extra love (and a sleep overnight).

make it veg/make it vegan
Some easy subs and ditched ingredients to make the recipe veg and/or vegan friendly.

gluten free
This indicates the recipe is already gluten-free, but feel free to sub in gluten-free flours, buns and pastas to other recipes.

spice it up
Yes sometimes I'm basic and tell you to add chilli, but spice it up can mean a lot of things. Some miso, curry paste or even chipotle sauce. I'll let you know if I think it can take the heat or a new flavour.

jazz it up
Making it a little more special. There's no need to crack open the caviar, but these tips can have the recipe dressed for a black-tie event or just a gathering of humans with a taco corner and endless margs.

m8s with
I'll let you know who's m8s with who. Some of these recipes can get a little cliquey so I thought it best to do the introductions.

use it up
Recipe-tailored tips for clearing the crisper or pantry to make sure nothing goes to waste.

prep ahead
I'll pop this in when I think it might be worth getting something going early on. I'm all about prepping ahead and cooking smart not hard!

meat lovers
I understand sometimes you need a bit more protein so I've popped this in when I think it might be worth adding a little extra meat.

more veg please
Some more of the good stuff. This will give you some ideas of how to get more veg in the recipe.

no fry
I get it – sometimes you'd prefer to not have loads of leftover oil to deal with. I'll give some options for not frying with this one.

YOU'VE GOT ENOUGH ON YOUR PLATE

So I thought we'd make things even more convenient and scale the recipes. This is not to say any of these recipes are hard – it's the opposite really, cos none of them make it to 5 – but I thought it was a good way of indicating how much you'll need to be involved in the process. I could have done a similar scale for flavour, but it's safe to say they'd all be getting 5s! Please don't use this scale as an excuse to not COOK ME, if anything it should give you more of an indication of when you can COOK ME as you'll be able to time accordingly. Gosh, sooo helpful. Here it is:

05

Lots of elements to cook or lots of chopping, you'll need another coffee to tackle these. Just kidding! As if any of these recipes are in here! I just wouldn't do that to you. But we'll keep it in to help to make sense of the scale.

04

Usually means there's one biggish job in there like cutting apples or slicing bulk onions that could take more than 5 minutes, or god forbid, making pastry from scratch. Alternatively I'm having you rest or chill something, which when you think about it requires zero effort, but I value your time so it's a 4 from me.

03

This is that sweet spot on the scale. Might be a bit of chopping involved, maybe an electric appliance. Maybe two pans or an oven and a stove come into play but it's nothing you can't handle. It's really an annoying score that gives you zero reasons not to COOK ME.

02

A super-straightforward recipe with quite minimal need to come up for air. Should be max 2–3 elements involved. Super easy to get into a rhythm with these recipes. Basically some chopping, heat and a few pans (some people also call this 'cooking').

01

So simple, the ingredients are doing a lot of the work for you and you're just there to fluff the pillows and make them look pretty. Regardless, the end result will be fab and quite effortless. You could say this recipe could be done easily first thing on a Monday without coffee – but what mad person would even test that theory.

THE
1–5
SCALE

TIPS & TRICKS

Confidence in the kitchen starts with having a solid base of ingredients and equipment. Here are some savvy ideas and lists to help you get cooking with ease . . .

SHOPPING KNOW-HOW

I'm not here to tell you how to shop, but I am here to stress how important the shop is. Whenever I move to a new city or area, I first get a good bearing on where the best shops are. Now I'm not just talking your basic supermarket, I'm talking veggie shop, butcher, deli, health-food shop, sourdough bakery, fishmonger, cake-supply shop, Indian grocer, Middle Eastern grocer, Asian grocers, including Chinese, Korean, Japanese . . . It's this food map that anchors what and when I'll cook something.

I like to think of food shopping as visiting 'food museums' (when I talk to my one-year-old daughter, that is). She loves heading to all the different museums to get the yummy things. I know if I'm planning on getting coriander chutney, which is in the frozen section at the Indian grocer, I'm surely also going to get a bulk pack of frozen naan, a packet of Kashmiri chilli powder, some curry leaves and maybe some more basmati rice. No doubt about it. And with that I already have a few recipes up my sleeve for the future. It's similar to that feeling you get having multiple cans of tomatoes in the pantry (and don't tell me you don't know what that is). Cooking starts with pantry and freezer confidence – and to have that, you gotta know how to shop.

To do this, it's about shopping for future you and creating a solid base – cos I'm all about that base. By utilising both the pantry and the freezer and having things at your fingertips we're solid from the get-go, making the cooking the easy part. Again, I stress work smart not hard; it's this foundation that will mean there's nothing stopping you from cooking 'that' recipe, but also makes the cooking more exciting.

Throughout the recipes I pull out and explain some special ingredients. And yes they are special – I'd add them to my birthday guest list if I could.

My way of cooking relies heavily on full-bodied, delicious, good-quality ingredients. The right ingredient can be a game changer to a recipe as they can do half the job for us – it's about putting the best in so you get the best out. Here's a look at a typical shopping list, including need-to-haves as well as nice-to-haves, as well as where to buy them, to help you through. (Plus a few extra tips.)

NEED-TO-HAVES

ARTISAN BAKERY
• good-quality sourdough

SUPERMARKET
Fridge
• milk
• cheese: a block of basic Tasty, a melty-style gruyère or mozzarella, and a hard style: pecorino or Parmesan
• butter: block, spreadable and garlic
• yoghurt: Greek-style

Pantry
• flaky salt and mixed peppercorns for the pepper grinder
• extra virgin olive oil (the big bottle treat it as an investment in yourself)
• whole-egg mayo and Kewpie mayo
• dill pickles
• sauerkraut (I love the shelf-stable version, but you can get it in the fridge section too)
• canned tomatoes
• tonic water: look, no recipes in the book use this but you can use your imagination to see why it's necessary (see limes)
• peanut butter: smooth or crunchy, mood dependent
• maple syrup: the real stuff only (again, an investment)
• pasta: long and short

• noodles: one or two varieties
• rice: basmati, jasmine, short and long grain (even a few microwave options if they're on special!)
• canned tuna
• canned beetroot
• tomato paste
• vinegar: apple cider, sherry, white wine, red wine, balsamic
• flour: self-raising, plain and strong (used for bread)
• canned beans and legumes
• block of chocolate (sorry, had to)

Freezer
• frozen peas and corn
• store-bought pastry
• ice cream (obvs)

Fruit and veggies
• garlic
• onions: brown, red, leeks, French shallots, spring onion
• lemons and limes
• free-range eggs (I put these in with the veggies cos they're always in a weird spot)
• plus whatever is on sale fruit and veggie wise – usually means it's in season

Spices
Where do I start, can you just get them all? I don't know what mood I'll be in but the super essentials are:
• smoked paprika: Gives a depth of heat without being hot, then the smoky element brings out the Texas BBQ vibe we sometimes need to get quickly into food without having to organise a smoker and wood chips
• ground cumin and coriander: These two work well together, kinda like

tomatoes and basil. Go heavy on one or the other to give either an earthy (cumin) or grassy (coriander) overtone. These do well in Mexican-style dishes, curries, and into sauces to pull out the underground savoury tones you're striving for
• ground turmeric: Always use with a little cracked pepper as it helps bring out the turmeric taste. Turmeric is a great colour adder for yellow tones (watch your fingers; she can be brutal)
• ground cinnamon: The ultimate spice. Check how strong yours is when you buy it and adjust accordingly. Cinnamon is perfect for making anything taste like love has been added and goes with most baked goods, and apples (always)
• ground nutmeg: A savoury and sweet spice that, thanks to being used in béchamel (white sauce), can give the aura of cheesiness when used in savoury cooking. A small amount goes a long way with this one and it can be bought as a whole piece and freshly grated!
• dried oregano: I used to hate dried oregano but now I find it slipping back into a lot of my cooking. A flavour builder that spans cuisines and gives the undertones of grassy herbyness many savoury dishes do well with
• chilli flakes: The spice of life. If toasted they come with a bit more heat! When scattered to finish they add a beautiful almost edible glitter vibe that lends a mild heat to the dish

NICE-TO-HAVES

BUTCHER
- bacon and other cured meats
- chicken bones for stock
- good-quality sausages

MIDDLE EASTERN GROCER
- dried chickpeas
- pomegranate molasses: A sticky, thick, sour syrup made from pomegranate juice and rich molasses. Has a beautiful gloss that adds a unique richness to simple dishes
- ras-el-hanout: A Middle Eastern spice blend that translates in Arabic to 'top shelf'. It can include more than 12 different spices with different balances of heat. The best usually feature a combo of cardamom, cumin, clove, cinnamon, nutmeg, mace, allspice, dry ginger, chili, coriander, peppercorn, sweet and hot paprika, fenugreek and turmeric. I like to add a little more turmeric when I use it as a rub so it has a beautiful colour
- baharat: A spice blend which is used for both savoury and sweet dishes, and is usually a combination of cinnamon, nutmeg, ginger, fenugreek, allspice, pepper and cloves
- tahini: A sesame paste. Think smooth peanut butter, but made with sesame seeds – either hulled or unhulled. I tend to use hulled tahini for the lighter colour but they are interchangeable in recipes
- za'atar: The name for a wild hyssop, and also the name of a herb and spice blend that traditionally features that herb – alongside things like sesame seeds, cumin, coriander and sumac
- garlic toum: A blitzed garlic paste made with lemon juice, garlic, oil and salt. If you love garlic, this is spreadable gold! Use smeared onto wraps or served with grilled meats
- golden raisins

ASIAN GROCER
- sriracha: A chilli sauce used to add a kick to a dish. Also called 'rooster sauce', cos of the rooster on the bottle. And yes it totally goes well with chicken
- chilli crisp: A chilli-infused oil with the chilli left in for crunch. Usually not super spicy but a good level of heat with a rich red oil for spooning over dishes. Peanut chilli crisp is also on high rotation at my house
- crispy fried shallots
- miso (red and white)
- kimchi
- gochujang: A fermented red chilli paste
- frozen dumplings
- frozen udon noodles
- Japanese pickled ginger
- Chinese black vinegar: An aged rice vinegar that has a malty almost caramel flavour to it
- Kewpie: an egg yolk- and soy-based mayo, named after the Kewpie dolls of Japan popular at the time it was invented
- rice vinegar
- shichimi togarashi: A Japanese spice blend of chilli flakes, sesame seeds and seaweed
- frozen/fresh pandan leaves: Pandan leaves are from the tropical pandanas plant and are used to flavour. Similar to how you might use a cinnamon stick, it gives a flavour almost similar to a grassy tea with notes of vanilla and coconut
- edamame
- frozen/fresh roti
- bonito flakes: Dried bonito fish thinly sliced into shavings and used as the base to make dashi and miso soup. A staple ingredient in Japanese cuisine
- Thai curry pastes
- hoisin

INDIAN GROCER
- frozen naan
- ghee
- Kashmiri chilli powder: An impressively red chilli powder that's mild in flavour but colours everything it touches with a beautiful red hue. Used similarly to the way turmeric is used to achieve a yellow colour
- nigella seeds

- tandoori paste
- eggplant chutney/kasundi:
  A sticky, sweet, and sour
  chutney made with eggplant,
  spices and tamarind. Perfect
  to finish a dish that needs
  a sour-sweet element or
  smeared into pastries or
  onto toast
- frozen coriander/mint
  chutney: A fresh product
  made by blitzing fresh
  coriander or mint with ginger,
  green chilli, garlic, lemon
  juice and cumin or chaat
  masala to create a beautiful
  green sauce. Found in the
  frozen section to keep it
  fresh, just thaw in your fridge
  before using or scrape, like
  you would a granita, and
  combine with yoghurt for the
  perfect dipping sauce. Can
  be quite spicy so taste first to
  know how much to use
- curry leaves
- date and tamarind chutney:
  Used in Indian cuisine, the
  natural sweetness of the date
  and the sour nature of the
  tamarind work in harmony
  for a rich, spiced, jammy
  puree to be spooned over
  anything crunchy, deep fried
  or bland to take it to a whole
  new level of yum! Perfect with
  potatoes, yoghurt, chickpeas,
  fresh herbs and yoghurt

SUPERMARKET
- good-quality choc chips
- caramelised onion relish
- sesame seeds
- instant mash/dehydrated
  potato
- anchovies
- pickled onions

- horseradish
- chicken salt
- buttermilk
- BBQ and tomato sauces

DELI/GROCER
- pâté
- porcini mushroom powder:
  Made from dried porcini
  mushrooms, a full-flavoured
  mushroom. Essentially I like
  to think of it as stock powder
  for vegetarians and vegans,
  as it adds a rich umaminess
  to anything it goes in
- Greek dried oregano
- Parmesan rinds (freeze what
  you don't use)
- harissa: A North African chilli
  sauce or spice mix that can
  be bought or made fresh with
  roasted chillis, garlic, olive oil
  and spices or as a dry spice
  mix using spices like chilli,
  cumin, coriander, paprika,
  caraway and garlic powder
- preserved lemon: Lemon
  wedges that have been
  preserved in salt so that
  the rind becomes soft and
  tender. Perfect in a slow
  braise or finely chopped and
  stirred through sauces for a
  different layer of citrus
- taramasalata: A Greek dip
  made with tarama, which is
  a salted and cured roe of cod
  or carp, found in a can
  in Greek delis
- marinated olives
- fresh mozzarella
- cheese (various varieties)
- dill pickles
- cornichons or French pickles:
  Small, sweet baby cucumber
  pickles in a sweet and sour
  brine with dill and spices

IF IT'S ON SALE, GRAB IT AND FREEZE IT
- makrut lime leaves
- lemongrass
- hot smoked salmon
- Lebanese bread
- naan
- fresh roti
- curry leaves

Hawt
tip!

Need a shopping list for
the recipe? Most smart
phones will let you take
a photo of the text of the
recipe. Once you've got
the snap on your phone,
use your finger to highlight
over the ingredient text list.
Press 'Copy', then open
your notes or messages to
yourself and press 'Paste'.
Boom! Shopping list ready
to go go. Genius, right? I'm
calling it the #listie. It's the
new selfie people, so get
amongst it.

It should be said, though:
Shopping lists are great,
but please be open to what
is seasonal and available.
Let that guide what goes
into the pie or the noodles.
These recipes are meant
to be flexible and
adaptable to what you
have and what's available
– cos that also usually
means it's cheaper, too!

SOME LOVE FOR THE FREEZER & FRIDGE

There's nothing wrong with being fridge and freezer obsessed. I take pride in the shelves of my fridge and freezer, which probably says a lot about me as a person . . .

One of my biggest tips for working smart at home is to buy a roll of masking tape and a sharpie pen. Boom, you have yourself a label maker.

Bolognese? Date it, label it, into the freezer.

Pickles? Date it, label it, and into the fridge (right at the back where it will be forgotten but you won't mind cos there's a label on it telling you exactly what it is).

I take things even further and like to have a stocktake sheet that sits on the freezer door. Nothing worse than freezing your fingers off digging for that thing you can't remember but you know it's in there! Instead, whenever something goes in the freezer give it a little blurb on your sheet, label your container with your sharpie, and you got yourself an almost freezer menu!

KITCHEN SPOILERS & EQUIPMENT TO KEEP IN MIND

Spoiler alert, Australia! Most of the world have different tablespoon measures! In Australia, a standard tablespoon measure is 20ml, or 4 teaspoons. In the US, UK and New Zealand, however, a tablespoon holds 15ml, or 3 teaspoons. It's such a nightmare. Where it will make a huge difference in the recipes, I have used teaspoon measures instead of tablespoons to be safe and to be sure you get the right amount.

Try and use a 15ml tablespoon measure where you can, cos sorry Australia but that is what the rest of the world uses and actually makes a lot of sense. But if you only have a 20ml tablespoon I've made sure you're safe.

Ovens . . . I always cook in a fan-forced oven, because the fan and element combo keeps the heat consistent and efficient. But if you have a convection oven, whereby the elements on the top and bottom run without a fan, just increase the temperature by 20°C. Therefore, if a recipe says 200°C fan forced, set your convection oven to 220°C.

Below is a list of utensils that are handy to have in the kitchen:

NEED-TO-HAVES
- box grater
- measuring scales
- measuring cups
- table- and teaspoon measures (preferably a 15ml tablespoon measure)
- large non-stick frypan
- sharp big knife – treat yourself and keep it sharpened
- small serrated knife
- julienne peeler – you can find these in kitchen supply shops; they look like a speed peeler but with teeth over the blade to make it slice and julienne

NICE-TO-HAVES
- microplane – finely grates zest and cheese and is perfect for mincing garlic
- stick blender
- mandolin – a vegetable slicer that cuts things super thin easily
- stand mixer – great for doughs, cake beating and if you can upgrade to have the pasta attachment, I thoroughly recommend it
- food processor – big and small
- slow cooker – I have two, they're that handy; like another set of hands
- grill pan
- heavy-based lidded saucepan
- coffee machine (lol at me having this in here but truly I think it's such a must)

If you use the imperial system in your kitchen, go to page 301 for a handy conversion chart.

From samwiches, to schnitties, cakes to crumbles, this is a cookbook of food stuffed to the absolute brim with flavour while also scaled in the amount of effort required. It's a choice sensation, ready to fit in with you – cos I think you're amazing.

LET'S GET COOKING

DIP

You'll always find me by the food at a party, and I'm an absolute sucker for a dip. I think it's the balance of something creamy and crisp to scoop it up with, but also how it's laid out before you literally screaming EAT ME.

SLAP IT TOGETHER

ulitimate
avo dip
(pg 28)

GO TO

cheesy onion
french stix
(pg 30)

LONG GAME

loaded meatball
hummus
(pg 32)

ultimate avo dip

I got introduced to this dip when I first started dating Luke. (Spoiler alert: we're married now.) Always brought out at family BBQs, it's hard to leave any room for mains once you get chomping on this dip of layers. This is the ultimate bring-a-plate option.

effort 1/5	veg	gluten free	serves 6–8 as a starter	prep 10 min

250g sour cream
1 (30g) sachet taco seasoning
  (who knows what's in this stuff but
  man it makes everything tasty
  right?! Alt. use the spice mix from
  the pork burgers on page 58)
4 avocados, peeled and de-stoned
juice of 1 lime, plus extra wedges
  to serve
3 vine-ripened tomatoes, diced
1 bunch spring onion, sliced
200g Cheddar, freshly grated
smoked paprika and corn chips,
  to serve

Mix sour cream and taco seasoning in a bowl.

Mash avo with lime juice roughly.

Spoon sour cream onto a serving platter, add avo, then scatter with tomato, spring onion and grated cheese.

Scatter with paprika and serve with corn chips and lime wedges.

spice it up	A good glug of chipotle hot sauce in the sour cream mixture and some jalapeños!	jazz it up	With a frozen margarita or two.	m8s with	Mincey burritos with cheesy rice and beans (page 116) – now that's a fiesta I can get behind.

cheesy onion french stix

Whoever thought of turning a whole loaf of bread into a serving dish for a dip is a magician if you ask me. This dip will change your life – big call, I know, but it's that delicious. And as my mother-in-law says: 'There's always room for bread.'

effort 1/5	veg	serves 8–10 as a starter	prep 5 min	cook 20–25 min

2 half-size baguettes or any bread
   you're happy to dive into
250g cream cheese, chopped
250g sour cream
½ cup (140g) store-bought
   caramelised onion or relish
1 (30g) sachet French onion soup mix
150g grated mozzarella cheese
150g frozen spinach, thawed and
   drained
2 tbsp finely grated Parmesan
chives, to garnish
potato chips to serve (salt and
   vinegar chips work crazy well here)
olive oil for drizzling

Preheat oven to 170°C fan forced . Grease and line a baking tray with baking paper.

Cut the tops off the baguettes with a serrated knife and slice into pieces, then transfer to the prepared tray. Hollow out the baguette inner and tear into dip-size pieces and transfer to tray.

Place cream cheese, sour cream, caramelised onion and soup mix in the bowl of a food processor and whiz until smooth and combined. Fold through cheese and spinach.

Pour mixture into baguettes. Scatter with Parmesan, place towards the top of the oven and bake for 20–25 minutes or until golden. Scatter with chives and drizzle with olive oil. Serve warm with potato chips and bread pieces for dipping.

m8s with	The sticky harissa glazed salmon (page 162), iceberg chunk salad (page 176) and a bottle of Chardonnay.	jazz it up	Ditch the bread and bake dip mixture in an ovenproof dish, then serve with bread sticks for a fondue vibe.

loaded meatball hummus

I could have stopped with just hummus, but it made sense to give you the whole shebang. Juicy meatballs piled onto creamy hummus – this is comfort food at its finest. This makes a large batch of hummus, so plenty for leftovers.

effort 4/5	serves 4, or 12 as a starter	prep 30 min	cook 1 hr	begin recipe 1 day ahead

⅓ cup (70g) golden raisins*
2 tbsp sherry vinegar
400g lamb mince
1 tbsp ras-el-hanout*
1 small red onion, grated
2 tbsp olive oil
400g can chopped tomatoes
50g butter
½ bunch parsley, finely chopped
toasted pine nuts, sumac and
  toasted pita to serve

Hummus
2 cups (370g) dried chickpeas*
1 tsp bicarb soda
1 carrot, chopped
1 brown onion, chopped
6 garlic cloves + 3 extra
½ cup (125ml) extra virgin olive oil
1 tbsp ground cumin
⅓ cup (90g) hulled tahini
juice of 3 lemons

*Specialty ingredients
Golden raisins, ras-el-hanout and dried chickpeas can be found at a Middle Eastern grocer. While you're there pick up some flat bread, olives and labneh, and you've sorted yourself for breakfast, too.

Soak raisins overnight in sherry vinegar.

Soak chickpeas and bicarb soda in a saucepan overnight.

The next day, begin to make the hummus by bringing the saucepan of chickpeas to the boil. Then drain and rinse chickpeas and return to pot with carrot, onion and garlic and fill three-quarters with water. Bring to the boil, skimming off the foam that comes to the top, and cook for 35 minutes or until chickpeas are tender and squish when pressed with a fork. Drain, reserving liquid, and return pan to low heat with oil and cumin and cook for 3–4 minutes, stirring, until aromatic. Remove from heat and add tahini, extra garlic, lemon juice, 5 ice cubes and chickpeas. Use a stick blender to blend until smooth, adding more of the reserved cooking water if needed until you get the right smooth consistency. Season to taste. Alternatively, transfer to a blender and puree in batches. Transfer to a container and chill until required.

For the meatballs, combine mince, ras-el-hanout and onion in a bowl. Roll tablespoons of mixture between wet hands and chill until required.

Heat oil in a frypan over medium heat. Add the meatballs and cook, rolling to seal all over, for 4–5 minutes, or until evenly browned. Add tomatoes and quarter of a cup water (use to rinse out the can) and bring to the boil. Add the butter and most of the raisin mixture, reserving a handful for garnishing, and simmer for 10–15 minutes, or until liquid is reduced and meatballs are cooked through. Season to taste.

Spoon hummus onto a serving dish. Spoon over lamb meatballs and scatter with chopped parsley. Finish with pine nuts, remaining raisins and sumac. Serve with pita alongside for dipping.

 make it vegan Ditch the meatballs and butter, and make it a beautiful raisin tomato sauce – you won't know the difference.

 prep ahead Hummus freezes like a dream! I transfer to containers and add a layer of oil to the top, then freeze. It will keep for up to 3 months.

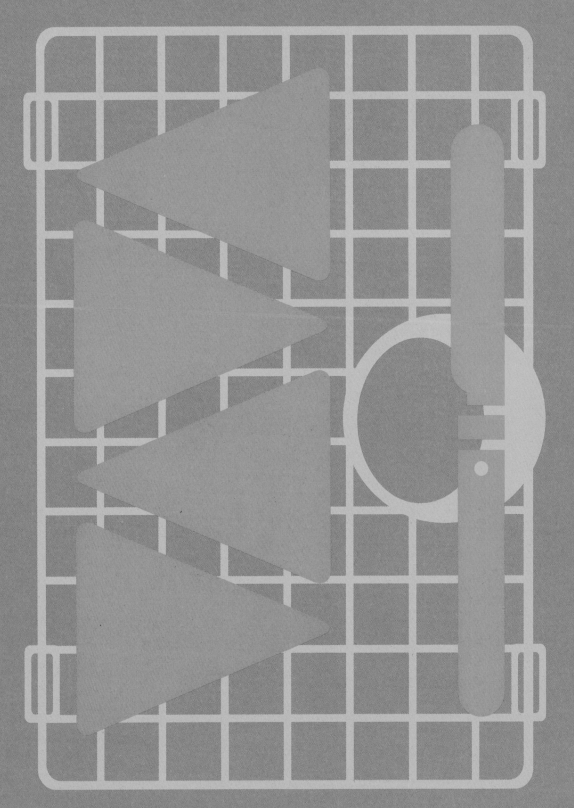

SAVO-URY SCHNAX

I am here for the schnax. The cabinet of a café will always have my heart, but also my wallet cos I can never say no to a freshly baked cheese scone. The aroma! *chefs kiss*.

SLAP IT TOGETHER
the cheesiest scone that ever lived
(pg 38)

GO TO
fennel sausage rolls
(pg 40)

LONG GAME
curry butter snails with spinach and feta
(pg 42)

3-2-1 SCONE!

A clash with a box grater, some hand gestures, a schmear of buttermilk and a shimmy with a knife and you've got yourself a cheeeeeeesy scone. Shiza, that looks super simps. Turn the page for the actual recipe with actual measurements for when you actually COOK ME and actually eat me – like, actually.

THE CHEESIEST SCONE THAT EVER LIVED
STEP X STEP

1. Combine flour and other dry things on a clean work surface.

2. Grate in the cheese, butter and chopped greens. By grating, we keep the cheese and butter cold without over-handling it.

3. Use the fingertips to smooch the flour and create something close to a breadcrumb texture – best to use fingertips only, cos the palms of our hands are hawt.

4. Create a well and add buttermilk and relish to the centre.

5. Use a butter knife to cut into the dough and incorporate the wet and the dry.

6. Once semi-incorporated, start using your hands to bring it together and briefly knead.

7. Shape into a disc.

8. Brush with buttermilk.

9. Cut into 8 triangles (the circle helps keep the pieces even).

10. Transfer to a lined baking tray.

11. Scatter with extra cheese and dollop with cream cheese (the game-changing ingredient – feel free to add more if you like it extra cheesy).

12. Bake until golden and tuck in! (Butter compulsory.)

the cheesiest scone that ever lived

I'd say this is my most eaten food since moving to New Zealand. Only eaten warm with lashings of butter. These cheese scones are undeniably some of the most delicious carb- and cheese-loaded goodies you'll ever have the pleasure of baking. I wish I had a personal chef to make them for me every day. Thank you New Zealand for sharing this delicious café schnack with me. See previous page for a step-by-step demo.

 effort 3/5 veg makes 8 prep 15 min cook 15–20 min

3 cups (450g) self-raising flour
200g grated Cheddar, plus 50g
  extra to scatter
100g butter, grated, plus extra
  to serve
handful finely chopped green things
  (totes optional, you could use
  parsley or chives)
½ tsp baking powder
½ tsp white pepper
1 tsp flaky salt
1½ cups (375ml) buttermilk, plus
  2 tbsp extra for brushing
2 tbsp caramelised onion relish
100g cream cheese, cut/divided
  into 8 pieces

Preheat oven to 210°C fan forced and line a baking tray with baking paper.

Combine flour, cheese, butter, green things, baking powder, white pepper and salt in a large bowl. Use fingertips to rub together slightly. Add buttermilk and relish and use a knife to cut through mixture then lightly knead to form a ball. Add more milk if you think it needs it.

Transfer to a lightly floured work surface and press out to a 20cm disc. Brush with extra buttermilk and cut evenly with a sharp knife into 8 even triangles. Transfer to prepared tray, add cream cheese to each piece and scatter with extra cheese.

Bake for 20–25 minutes, or until cooked through and golden.

Serve warm with lashings of butter.

 jazz it up Cut and top each half with bacon or salmon and serve with a poached egg and hollandaise sauce for a cheesy Benedict.

 prep ahead For a quick scone, have the crumbled flour, cheese, butter and green thangs ready to go in the fridge. That way, first thing in the morning you can add the wet thangs and baking powder and pop them straight into the oven for fresh baked scones – with even less fuss.

fennel sausage rolls

These fennel-forward pastries are sure to please a crowd – unless they're vegetarian, in which case see below for some options. There's something so nostalgic about a sausage roll. As they say, 'it's a long way to the shop if you want a sausage roll', so you might as well cook your own.

 effort 2/5   makes 16   prep 10 min   cook 25–30 min

400g fresh, good-quality sausages (pick your fave, mine are Italian)

1 cup (100g) coarsely grated fennel

2 tbsp tomato relish, plus extra to serve

1 tbsp caramelised onion relish

2 tsp fennel seeds, crushed

2 tbsp each breadcrumbs and instant mash/dehydrated potato flakes*

1 egg, plus 1 extra yolk for brushing

2 sheets ready-rolled frozen puff pastry, thawed

1 tbsp each sesame and poppy seeds

*Specialty ingredients
Instant mash/dehydrated potato flakes is one of my fave ingredients, as it's a handy way of bringing a softness and starch to any filling. A great secret pantry-weapon! Make sure to check the ingredients list on the packet – we want to only see one ingredient: potatoes.

Preheat oven to 220°C fan forced and line a large baking tray with baking paper.

Slit sausage casings and squeeze out filling onto a plate. If you're as immature as me, this can be awkward – sorry in advance.

Place sausage filling, fennel, tomato relish, caramelised onion, fennel seeds, breadcrumbs, instant mash and egg. Mix well with hands, squishing until combined.

Cut the pastry sheets in half. Spoon a line of the pork mixture along one long edge of each pastry piece. Roll the pastry over to enclose the filling. Cut each roll into 4. Place onto prepared tray.

Brush the sausage rolls with egg yolk and sprinkle with sesame and poppy seeds. Reduce oven to 200°C and bake for 25–30 minutes, or until golden brown. Serve with extra tomato relish.

 make it veg
Sub the sausage with cooked sweet potato and a can of cannellini beans, mashed. Throw in some breadcrumbs to get the right – not so sloppy – consistency, which holds its own when put on pastry.

 prep ahead
Make these sausage rolls up and wrap in baking paper, then freeze. Cook from frozen, brushed and seeded, for 35–40 minutes or until cooked through. Then cut to serve.

curry butter snails
with spinach and feta

I wanted a savoury snail, but with a nod towards its raisin-laden brother. Brushing curry butter in the layers, crumbling both feta and paneer for the filling, and finishing with the tamarind chutney creates the sweet and savoury balance we're looking for in this tasty escargot.

effort 3/5 · veg · makes 6 · prep 30 min · cook 35–40 min

200g spinach leaves (or half spinach, half silver beet)
200g Danish feta, crumbled
200g paneer*, crumbled
½ tsp ground white pepper
2 eggs
150g ghee*, melted
3 tsp curry powder
2 tbsp date and tamarind chutney*, plus extra to serve
18 sheets (approx. 1 packet) filo pastry
20 curry leaves*

Specialty ingredients
Paneer, ghee, date and tamarind chutney and curry leaves can all be found at a good Indian grocer – one of my favourite places to shop. Keep an eye out for the frozen naan and some Kashmiri chili powder while you're there: two birds, one stone.

Preheat oven to 200°C fan forced. Grease and line a baking tray or baking dish with baking paper.

Put spinach onto tray and bake (as oven is heating up is fine) for 5 minutes, or until slightly wilted. Combine in a bowl with feta, paneer, pepper, 1 egg and 1 egg white, reserving egg yolk. Combine ghee, curry powder and tamarind chutney in a separate bowl.

On a clean work surface, lay out 1 sheet of filo and brush with curry butter. Repeat twice more, so you have a stack of 3 filo sheets. Put one-sixth of the filling mixture along one long side of the pastry and roll away from you to make a long sausage. Brush edges lightly with water to make it more flexible and shape into a snail. Transfer to baking tray. Repeat with remaining pastry and filling. Brush all snails again with any remaining butter, then brush with reserved egg yolk and scatter with curry leaves. Bake for 30–35 minutes or until golden and crisp. Serve with extra chutney.

jazz it up
Turn this into one BIG snail to serve to a crowd so people can nip off as much as they like. Bake it in a round dish, and keep adding to the coil of the first pastry from the middle to reach the edges of the dish.

use it up
Fresh spinach is great but if you want to sub in a mixture of frozen thawed spinach, or some herb ends like parsley and dill, it's a great way of getting rid of some annoying end bits of greenery from the crisper.

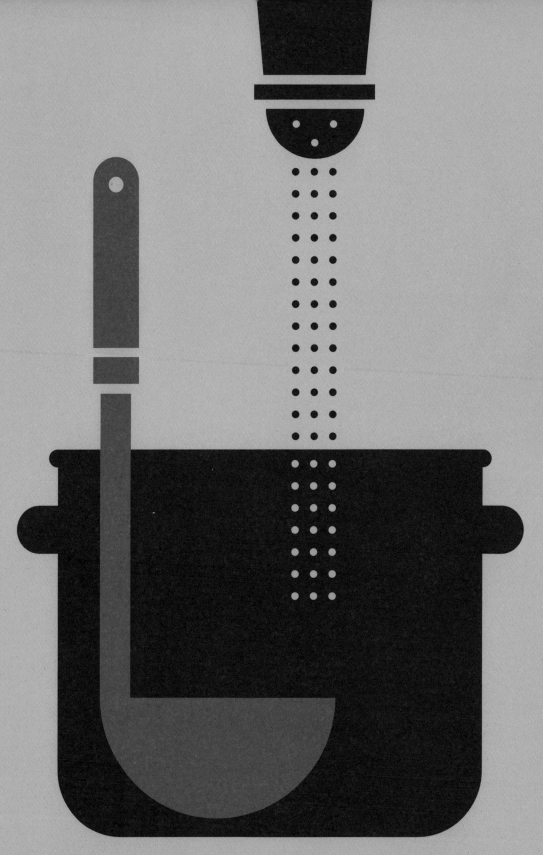

SOUP

Bowls of yum – you could give me soup any day of the year and I'd be a happy lady. But make sure it comes with something crusty to dip into, or is filled with noodles to slurp up.

SLAP IT TOGETHER

pumped miso ginger pumpkin soup
(pg 46)

GO TO

roast cauliflower soup with squishy garlic parmesan toast
(pg 48)

LONG GAME

french onion and sauerkraut soup with cheesy garlic bread
(pg 50)

pumped miso ginger pumpkin soup

This soup is PUMPED with flavour. The pickled ginger addition is genius if you ask me. Everything in a pot to cook then a whiz with a stick blender and she's ready for eating. You'll be craving this even in the peak of summer – it's that good!

effort 2/5 · veg · serves 4–6 · prep 5 min · cook 25–35 mins

1 brown onion, finely chopped
2 garlic cloves , bruised
1 tsp chilli crisp*, plus extra to serve
1 tbsp peanut oil
1 tsp sesame oil
¼ cup (75g) miso paste*
1kg peeled pumpkin, chopped into
    4cm pieces
2 tbsp bonito flakes*
1.25 litres (5 cups) of water
½ cup (125ml) cream
¼ cup (45g) pickled ginger* and
    2 tbsp pickling juice (essential
    flavour maker), plus extra to serve
shredded seaweed and shichimi
  togarashi*, to serve

*Specialty ingredients
Chilli crisp, miso paste, bonito
flakes, pickled ginger and shichimi
togarashi can be found at most
Asian supermarkets.

Place onion, garlic, chilli crisp and oils in a saucepan over medium heat and cook, stirring for 3–4 minutes or until softened slightly. Add miso, pumpkin, bonito flakes and water (enough to just cover). Bring to the boil then reduce heat to low, add cream and cook for 20–30 minutes, or until pumpkin is tender and cooked through.

Add ginger and pickling juice and puree with a stick blender or transfer in batches to a blender to puree. Taste for seasoning. Divide among bowls, top with extra chilli crisp, togarashi and shredded seaweed with extra ginger alongside.

make it vegan — Lose the bonito and chuck in some dried shiitake, then sub the cream with cashew cream or leave it out completely.

spice it up — A teaspoon of chilli powder thrown in with the onion at the beginning takes the spice up a notch if that's more your cup of soup.

roast cauliflower soup
with squishy garlic parmesan toast

This soup could have been as white as snow, but it is safe to say it would not have been as flavoursome. Roasting both the garlic and the cauliflower gives maximum flavour to this dish – and also shoving it all in the oven makes it minimal fuss. COOK ME. Taste me. This is my hug in a bowl. Tell me what you think.

 effort 2/5 veg serves 4–6 prep 10 min cook 1 hr

850g cauliflower, cut into 6 wedges (approx. 1 cauliflower)
2 brown onions, halved
½ bunch thyme, leaves picked
¼ cup (60ml) olive oil, divided
50g butter, chopped
2 garlic bulbs
1 litre chicken stock
200ml cream, plus extra to drizzle
4 slices sourdough bread, toasted
20g Parmesan, finely grated
½ bunch chives, finely chopped

Preheat oven to 180°C fan forced and grease and line a roasting tray with baking paper.

Put cauliflower, onion and thyme onto prepared tray and drizzle with 2 tablespoon oil and scatter over blobs of butter. Place garlic bulbs on a piece of foil and drizzle with 1 tablespoon of olive oil. Wrap to enclose. Add to tray.

Roast for 45 minutes, or until garlic has softened and is easy to squeeze from cases, and cauliflower is cooked through. Reserve some cauliflower for garnishing, then transfer remainder to a saucepan over high heat along with stock and cream. Bring to the boil then remove from heat and puree with a stick blender or transfer in batches to a blender to puree. Season to taste.

To make the squishy garlic Parmesan toast, squeeze garlic onto toast, discarding the skin, and scatter with Parmesan. Place in the oven for 5 minutes to melt slightly then serve with soup scattered with reserved cauliflower, chives and an extra drizzle of cream.

 jazz it up Truffle oil to finish this soup is a boujie addition I'm here for.

 meat lovers Finely chopped chorizo cooked with olive oil and spooned over the soup to finish is a fab way of taking this soup up a notch.

 prep ahead This soup freezes like a dream. Make bulk and freeze for the future.

french onion and sauerkraut soup
with cheesy garlic bread

French onion soup was one of the first dishes I learnt as a budding chef under the guidance of the one-and-only Frank Boulay. It's stayed with me ever since – the addition of the sauerkraut is all me, though. I love how it gives the soup a fermented tang and the strands of cabbage sit comfortably in the soup with their sliced onion companions. A tip for slicing onions: just slice them. There's no point trying to avoid the tears; they're all part of the process. Bon appétit!

effort 4/5 · veg · serves 4 · prep 15 min · cook 1 hr 15 min

2 tbsp extra virgin olive oil
50g butter
5 brown onions, thinly sliced
3 bay leaves
½ bunch thyme, leaves picked, plus
  extra to serve
4 garlic cloves, thinly sliced
2 tbsp plain flour
⅔ cup (160ml) dry sherry, or port
2 litres beef stock (the good stuff if
  you can, but I never say no to a
  stock cube)
1 cup (200g) sauerkraut*, plus
  2 tbsp liquid
1 stick store-bought garlic bread
150g grated gruyere cheese*

*Specialty ingredient
Sauerkraut is fermented cabbage with a destinctive sour flavour and tang. Gruyere cheese is super melty and almost 'gamier' in taste compared to your standard Cheddar.

Heat oil and butter in a large, lidded saucepan over medium heat. Add onions, bay leaves and most of the thyme and cook until onions start to sizzle. Cover and cook, stirring regularly, for 30 minutes or until onions are softened and translucent.

Remove lid and add garlic and cook for a further 5 minutes, or until aromatic and beginning to caramelise. Add flour and cook, stirring, for 2 minutes or until it begins to stick to the bottom of the pan. Increase heat to high and add sherry and bring to the boil. Cook, scraping the bottom of the pan with a wooden spoon, for 3 minutes, or until liquid is reduced by half. Add stock and return to the boil. Reduce heat to low and cook for 25 minutes, or until reduced by one third. Stir through sauerkraut liquid and season to taste.

Prepare garlic bread as per packet instructions.

Heat oven grill. Divide soup among heatproof bowls, or one heatproof serving dish and top with bread, sauerkraut and cheese. Grill for 5–10 minutes, or until the cheese has melted and oozed its way into the soup. Serve hawt.

meat lovers — Chop and sear 700g of chuck steak and transfer with soup to a slow cooker on low for 4 hours for a stewy beef and onion soup.

prep ahead — This soup, like a fine wine, gets better with age. Make in advance; it keeps for a 1 week in the fridge. Or freeze for future you.

BURG-ER

Sandwiched between two (sometimes three) golden buns, there's nothing quite like a burger. But let's be honest, it's all about the filling – cos as they say it's what's inside that counts. Get your mouth around these loaded burgers asap.

SLAP IT TOGETHER

big beet burger
(pg 54)

GO TO

beer-batter fish burgers with tartare iceberg slaw
(pg 56)

LONG GAME

loaded pulled pork brekkie burgers
(pg 58)

SLAP IT TOGETHER

big beet burger

Making burgers? No one puts beetroot in the corner. In fact they put them centre stage with a solo routine. These patties ensure beetroot is always invited to the party by having it smashed into the patty and also wedged into the layers. Lets call it a burger that's beetroot 'double-parked'.

| effort 3/5 | serves 4 | prep 15 min | cook 10 min |

500g beef mince
1 cooked beetroot or ½ a small raw
  beetroot, coarsely grated
1 tsp horseradish cream*
½ cup (70g) pickled onions, finely
  chopped
½ cup (125ml) mayo
2 tbsp BBQ sauce
2 tbsp tomato sauce
2 tsp American mustard
1 tbsp finely chopped dill
2 tbsp extra virgin olive oil
5 rashers streaky bacon
5 burger buns, halved (sesame seed
  topping preferred – cos yum)
lettuce leaves, sliced tomato, pickles
  and sliced canned beetroot to serve

*Specialty ingredient
Horseradish cream, which is found
near the mustard and keeps in your
fridge for ages.

Combine mince, beetroot, horseradish and half of the pickled onion in a bowl. Throw the mince against the side of the bowl a few times to activate the proteins. Divide into five (cos there's always someone who wants seconds) and roll between hands into balls. Press into 1cm-thick patties and chill (in the fridge – obvs) on a plate for 10 minutes.

Meanwhile combine mayo, sauces, mustard and dill.

Heat oil in large frypan and add burger patties and bacon and cook, turning halfway, for 5–6 minutes or until cooked through and golden.

To assemble burgers, spoon the combined sauces onto the tops and bottom of the buns. Add lettuce leaves, burger patty, bacon, tomato, pickles, remaining pickled onion and beetroot slices. Finish with a bun and serve asap!

 make it veg Sub the beef patty for the patty in ultimate veg sammy (page 102), leaving out the curry powder and subbing in the grated cooked or raw beetroot.

 prep smart These patties only do better if they're left to chill. So, if you can make them ahead of time, it will make dinner mere minutes away when you're short of time.

beer-batter fish burgers
with tartare iceberg slaw

Fish burgers are a reg at our house and that crunchy coating, silky mayo and fluffy bun are a match made in heaven. The slaw in this burger is a classic morph of two iconic burger ingredients: iceberg lettuce and pickles. I am allll about it.

effort 4/5   serves 4-6   prep 15 min   cook 10 min

1 cup (150g) self-raising flour
2 tbsp rice flour, plus ½ cup (75g) extra for dusting
1½ cups (375ml) beer*
1 tsp celery salt*
400g firm white fish (I used gurnard fillets, but flathead would also work well)
1 tsp chicken salt
2 tomatoes, thinly sliced
6 ciabatta buns
vegetable oil for deep frying

Tartare iceberg slaw
1 small red onion, finely sliced
juice and zest of 1 lemon
2 tbsp capers, chopped
8 cornichons (or any pickle), finely chopped, plus extra to serve
¼ iceberg lettuce, shredded
1 tbsp chopped dill
½ cup (150g) mayo

Specialty ingredient
I used hazy pale ale, which is a nice fruity beer, but you can use whatever beer you like. Celery salt is a handy seasoning that adds savoury flavours to a dish.

For the slaw, combine all ingredients except the mayo.

Line a baking tray with paper towel. Heat 5cm of oil in a wide saucepan or wok over medium-high heat until it reaches 180°C on a thermometer. (If you don't have a thermometer, a cube of bread will turn golden in 30 seconds when the oil is hot enough.)

For the batter, whisk together flours, beer and celery salt in a bowl. Put extra rice flour in a separate bowl and, working in batches, toss fish in rice flour, dredge through the batter, then add to hot oil. Cook for 3–4 minutes or until fish is cooked through and batter is golden and puffed. Transfer to prepared tray and scatter with some chicken salt. Continue with remaining fish fillets.

To assemble burgers, add mayo to slaw and mix to coat and combine. Divide among burger buns and top with fish and tomato slices. Skewer burgers, with an extra cornichon on top, to hold together, and serve.

---

jazz it up
This makes for a fun dinner-party vibe. Up the fish and get some extra condiments and even some tortillas going for a make-your-own fish taco and burger corner.

no fry
Ditch the batter and go for a crumb sitch. See the chicken schnitty (page 212) for some inspiration and bake these fish fingers for your burger instead.

loaded pulled pork brekkie burgers

Shredded melt-in-your-mouth pork balanced out with a hash brown and tomato and spinach (for health purposes only). The slow-cooker pork should be started the day before you wish to serve it, so make it ahead of a night out for an effortless brekkie the next day. Your future self will thank you. Apologies in advance for the awkward tears of utter happiness.

 effort 3/5   serves 4, with leftover pork   prep 20 min   cook 5–8 hr

4 frozen hash browns
4 eggs
oil for frying
4 burger buns
4 slices smoked cheese*
¼ cup (75g) aioli, plus extra to serve
60g baby spinach leaves
1 tomato, sliced

Slow-cooker pork
1.2kg boneless pork shoulder roast, netting and skin removed
¼ cup (70g) tomato paste
⅓ cup (80g) firmly packed brown sugar
2 tbsp onion powder
1 tbsp each smoked paprika, sweet paprika, garlic powder, dried oregano
2 tsp each flaky salt and cracked pepper
227g can crushed pineapple, in juice
1 cup (250ml) water
2 tbsp apple cider vinegar

Specialty ingredient
Smoked cheese, found near the Cheddar, adds another level of flavour (and that's always a good idea). You can sub with reg cheese.

For the slow-cooker pork, coat pork in tomato paste. Combine, sugar, powders, spices and salt and pepper in a bowl. Sprinkle over pork to coat meat completely. Transfer to slow cooker and add pineapple and water. Cook on the low setting overnight (8+ hours), or high for 5 hours, or until pork is tender and easily pulls with a fork.

Add apple cider vinegar and use two forks to pull meat. Stand, covered, on the warm setting until required.

When ready to serve, cook hash browns as per packet instructions and fry eggs with oil.

Preheat oven grill to high. Halve buns and place on a baking tray, cut side up. Place cheese slices on bun bottoms and grill for 5–10 minutes, or until cheese is melted and tops are toasted. Spoon aioli onto bun tops, spreading all the way to the edges.

Top the bun bottoms with pulled pork, spinach, tomato, hash brown, egg, a little more pork and burger tops.

 make it veg   Sub the pork for 2 cans of beans and 2 cans of young green jackfruit.

 m8s with   This makes great burritos, too! Check out the 'Wrap me' chapter (page 110) for some inspo.

PIE

Wrap me up in pastry and put me to bed. Pastry is this gal's best friend. Please note: I am also open to chocolate and bread competing for best friend status.

SLAP IT TOGETHER

fish filo pie (pg 62)

GO TO

smoky silver beet and tomato galette with pickle juice crust (pg 66)

LONG GAME

slow-cooker beef and bacon pies with chutney crust (pg 68)

fish filo pie

Fish filo pie – say that fast six times. What a mouthful, similar to the mouthfuls you'll be getting with this pie! Fish loves itself in a pie, all dressed up in a creamy blanket with a crispy garlic butter pastry as a hat. I mean, I'm already hook, line and sinker. This is essentially chowder in pie form and it's a total winner.

effort 3/5 · serves 4–6 · prep 10 min · cook 35 min

2 tbsp olive oil
150g speck* or bacon, cut into thin
  lardons
3 cloves garlic, finely chopped
1 small leek, white part only,
  thinly sliced
¼ bunch dill, leaves picked and
  chopped, stems finely chopped
¼ cup (35g) plain flour
1 chicken stock cube, crumbled
1 cup (120g) frozen peas
300ml thickened cream
900g firm fish fillets (I used cod and
  salmon), cut into 3cm cubes
250g smoked mussels*
12 sheets filo
100g garlic butter, melted

Specialty ingredient
*Speck is similar to prosciutto and is
a cured and smoked meat usually
using the belly. Smoked mussels you
can sub with hot smoked salmon
or just increase the speck sitch.
Anything smoked works well here.*

Preheat oven to 200°C fan forced.

Place oil, speck, garlic, leek and dill stems in a large cold frypan and place over medium heat. When speck begins to sizzle, cook, stirring, for 2–3 minutes or until leek is softened, but not coloured.

Add flour and cook, stirring, for 2 minutes or until sticking slightly. Add stock cube, peas and cream. Bring to the boil and cook, stirring occasionally, for 2 minutes or until slightly reduced. Season to taste. Fold through fish, mussels and dill leaves.

Roughly brush half of the filo sheets with some of the melted garlic butter and layer on top of each other. Lay over a 1.5-litre capacity pie dish or cake pan so it covers the base and sides of the pan with some overhang. Add fish mixture and use the back of a spoon to press down, then bring the filo overhang up and over the filling. Roughly brush the remaining filo sheets with remaining garlic butter and layer on top of each other. Halve pastry and scrunch and rip then cover the top of the pie, tucking filo into the sides of the pan to enclose the filling. Drizzle with any remaining butter.

Bake for 25–30 minutes or until golden and cooked through. Serve warm!

spice it up
Loose the speck, sub the cream for coconut cream and add 1 tbsp green or red curry paste – now you've got yourself a curry fish pie.

more veg please
Serve with mash potatoes, extra peas and honeyed carrots for some Nana nostalgia.

A HANDY PIE CHART

Pastry take a bow, you're truly a star act. At its core, pastry is a process of laminating and or combining flour with fat to build a dough that is crispy/layered/crumbly/crunchy or even silky when cooked. My go-to pastries at home are:

BUTTER PUFF

The superior version of store-bought puff – be mindful when buying puff pastry cos the other versions (just called 'puff pastry') are based on vegetable oils and just aren't the same. Laminated and flaky, this pastry is perfect for anything in need of flaky butteriness such as the fennel sausage rolls (page 40).

FILO

You can make this pastry yourself from scratch but wow, it's hard – store-bought is fine. Filo is super-thin sheets of pure pastry that allow us to use a brush to add the fat and do the lamination ourselves. Perfect for the curry butter snails with spinach and feta (page 42).

SHORTCRUST

Buttery, short, crumbly, kind of annoying to roll out. But worth it for the crumb factor. Perfect for quiche, or more specifically, mine (page 172).

DUMPLING/WONTON

Usually an egg-based pastry, found in Asian grocers. These are a great cheat for a quick ravioli or dumplings at home. Can also be sprayed with oil and baked in mini muffins trays for easy casings for a canapé. Try them with the pork larb (page 114).

PIE CRUST

A bit more flexible with a higher water content and big chunks of fat to keep the flaky vibe alive. See opposite page for a demo on how it's made.

SPRING ROLL

An oil- and water-based pastry, handy for anything you need to be super crispy! Great for using up leftovers in the form of a spring roll – anything can be a spring roll when you've got the pastry. Cabbage curry noodle spring rolls are a damn fine idea (page 74).

SMOKY SILVER BEET AND TOMATO PIE
WITH PICKLE JUICE CRUST STEP X STEP

(Turn the page for the actual recipe with measurements for getting this pastry rolled, baked and delivered)

1. Roll out the pastry to about 4mm thickness; it's good to see those big chunks of butter marbling through.

2. Transfer to a sheet of baking paper – just makes everything easier.

3. Make potato mixture and stir through some silver beet leaves and grated cheese.

4. Scatter pastry with remaining cheese to give our edges some cheesy crust. Add the potato mixture.

5. Scatter over the remaining silver beet leaves (yep, it looks like a lot, but it will shrink). Arrange tomatoes on top

6. Bring the sides up and over the filling, creasing and pressing on the sides to enclose well.

7. Brush around some egg wash so she gets a bit sticky.

8. Scatter the edges with caraway seeds and pour the remaining egg into the centre to let it slowly pool inside.

9. Once she's baked, cut with a serrated knife and you're good to go.

smoky silver beet and tomato galette
with pickle juice crust

This pastry is my ride or die, no questions asked. The zing you get from the brining liquid balances the richness of the butter. It's also a great no-waste trick and turns a galette full of vegetables into one of the tastiest things in the world. Please feel free to go seasonal with your veg choice, let Mother Nature guide you – but always keep father pickle juice lurking in the fridge. Should be said though, this is that recipe for *what the hell do I do with an entire bunch of silver beet or chard*. See previous page for a step-by-step demo.

| effort 4/5 | veg | serves 6–8 | prep 40 min | cook 1 hr |

20g butter, plus extra for greasing
1 brown onion, thinly sliced
2 garlic cloves, finely chopped
200g clean potatoes, coarsely grated
1 bunch silver beet or chard, stems
   removed and sliced, leaves shredded
150g coarsely grated smoked Cheddar*
2 tomatoes, sliced
1 egg, lightly whisked
1 tbsp caraway seeds

Pickle juice pastry
2 cups (300g) plain flour, plus
   extra to dust
200g butter, chopped
pinch of salt
¾ cup (180ml) pickle juice

*Specialty ingredient
Smoked Cheddar is found in all good supermarkets, and if you manage to find manuka-smoked Cheddar, high five to you.

Preheat oven to 200°C fan forced. Grease and line a baking tray with baking paper.

For the pastry, place flour, butter and salt in a bowl and rub in the butter until the mixture resembles coarse breadcrumbs. Add pickle juice and use a butter knife to bring together to form a crumbly dough. Transfer to a clean work surface and knead briefly then shape it into a disc. Lightly dust with flour then roll out to 4mm thickness. Transfer to prepared tray and chill until required.

To make the filling, place butter, onion and garlic in a lidded saucepan or frypan over medium-high heat and cook, stirring, for 3–4 minutes or until softened. Add potato and silver beet stems. Cover and cook, stirring halfway, for 5 minutes or until softened. Leave to cool for 5 minutes. Stir through a handful each of silver beet leaves and cheese.

To assemble, scatter pastry with remaining cheese. Add potato mixture, remaining silver beet leaves and tomatoes to the centre of the pastry, leaving a 4cm border. Fold over pastry edges and squeeze to enclose. Brush pastry with egg then pour remaining egg into the centre. Scatter with caraway seeds.

Bake for 45 minutes–1 hour, or until the base moves easily on the tray and it's golden on top. Set aside for 10 minutes to rest before cutting and serving.

 Sub the butter for a mixture of half coconut oil, half vegan spread, lose the egg and use vegan cheese.

 A spread of 'nduja (spreadable salami) on the base of this pie can take it to a whole other level. Or throw in some bacon for a meaty vibe.

slow-cooker beef and bacon pies
with chutney crust

Imagine having these passed around at the footy? The glazed crust on these takes the pastry to a whole other level. Cooked low and slow, the meat is super tender, bound to leave you wanting more!

effort 3/5   serves 4   prep 15 min   cook 4.5 hr

¼ cup (60ml) extra virgin olive oil
1kg chuck beef, cut into 3cm pieces
200g bacon, cut into lardons
⅓ cup (50g) plain flour
3 brown onions, thinly sliced
4 garlic cloves, thinly sliced
2 bay leaves
2 tbsp tomato paste
1 tsp cracked pepper
½ bunch thyme, leaves picked, plus
   extra to serve
330ml bottle of beer
1 beef stock cube, crumbled
1 cup (250ml) water
1 tbsp cornflour
2 sheets all-butter puff pastry*
1 egg yolk, whisked
¼ cup (70g) tomato chutney or relish,
   plus extra to serve

*Specialty ingredient
All-butter puff – remember it's important to check for butter puff pastry. The taste difference is chalk and cheese (or should I say butter).

Heat 1 tablespoon oil in a frypan. Toss beef, bacon and flour in a bowl with salt and pepper. Working in batches, add to pan and cook, turning, for 5 minutes, or until browned. Transfer to a bowl.

Add remaining oil and onions to the pan and cook for 4–5 minutes, or until softened. Add garlic, bay leaves, tomato paste, pepper and thyme and cook for 2 minutes, or until aromatic. Add beer and stock cube and bring to the boil then cook for 5 minutes, or until beer is reduced by half.

Transfer to a slow cooker along with the water and cook on low heat for 6 hours or overnight, or high for 3 hours, or until meat is tender and shreds when pushed with a fork. Take out half a cup of the cooking liquid, add cornflour, and stir to dissolve. Return liquid to the filling and mix to combine.

Meanwhile, preheat oven to 200ºC fan forced. Divide beef mix among 4 ovenproof pie dishes (500ml capacity).

Cut each sheet of pastry into 16 squares and use to arrange over filling, overlapping slightly and working into the edges to cover pies completely. Brush with egg yolk and bake for 30 minutes or until golden and bubbling. Brush over chutney and return to the oven for 5 minutes to glaze. Remove and serve with extra chutney alongside.

spice it up

Sub the tomato paste for 2 tbsp of curry powder and these turn into something with a little kick to them. Also feel free to swap the beer for more stock.

more veg please

Throw in some frozen peas and cooked potatoes before tucking these pies into bed with pastry.

NOO-DLE

Long luscious noodles dripping, sometimes swimming, in sauce and flavour. Need I say more?

SLAP IT TOGETHER

chilli crisp peanut udon noodles with dumplings (pg 72)

GO TO

cabbage curry noodles (pg 74)

LONG GAME

liquid gold chicken laksa (pg 76)

chilli crisp peanut udon noodles
with dumplings

This hits every taste bud for me. It's right up my alley with spice, chew, freshness and convenience. If there's once recipe I hope you cook from this book, it's got to be this one. Slurp slurp.

effort 1/5	serves 2	prep 5 min	cook 10 min

12 frozen dumplings*
   (my go-to is pork and prawn
   but veg are good too)
200g frozen udon noodles*
   (sub with 150g dried noodles)
2 tbsp crunchy peanut butter
2 tbsp Chinese black vinegar*
2 tbsp light soy sauce
2 tsp peanut chilli crisp oil, plus
   extra to serve
3 spring onions, sliced
1 cucumber, shredded

Specialty ingredients
Frozen dumplings and udon are found at all Asian grocers and also most supermarkets. Just make sure to buy dumplings specifically for boiling – the back of the packet should tell you. Chinese black vinegar, an aged rice vinegar that has a malty almost caramel flavour, can also be found here.

Bring a saucepan of water to the boil. Add dumplings and cook as per packet instructions, adding the noodles in the last 3 minutes of cooking. Drain, and reserve half a cup cooking liquid.

Place peanut butter, vinegar, soy and chilli crisp in a frypan over high heat with cooking liquid and cook, stirring, for 2 minutes or until combined.

Add noodles and dumplings and toss to coat. Transfer to bowls and top with spring onion and cucumber. Finish with extra chilli crisp, and serve.

jazz it up	Store-bought Peking duck or Chinese BBQ pork to finish is never a bad idea.

 more veg please Cut a head of broccoli into florets and throw him in when you add the noods.

cabbage curry noodles

Trust the amount of cabbage here – similar to spinach, it shrinks and wilts to half its size. Big shout out to the eggyness of the noods: not only does it give a great chew, it takes on the curry vibe like a champ.

effort 2/5	veg	serves 4–6	prep 10 min	cook 15 min

250g dried thin egg noodles (can sub for a vegan option)*
2 tbsp vegetable oil
1 tsp sesame oil
1 long red chilli, thinly sliced, plus extra to serve
4 garlic cloves, thinly sliced
8 shiitake mushrooms, thinly sliced
200g firm tofu, crumbled
550g white cabbage (about half of one), thinly shredded
1 carrot, shredded
1½ tbsp soy sauce
1 tbsp curry powder
¼ tsp white pepper
1 tbsp rice wine vinegar
½ cup (125ml) water
crispy fried shallots, to serve

Specialty ingredient
You can get egg noodles at most supermarkets but head to an Asian supermarket for endless choice, you can grab the crispy fried shallots here also.

Cook the noodles as per packet instructions, drain and set aside.

Heat a wok or a large frypan over high heat. Add oils, chilli and garlic and cook for 1–2 minutes, or until garlic is turning golden on the edges. Add mushrooms and tofu and cook, tossing regularly, for 5 minutes or until turning crisp and golden. Transfer some to a bowl for scattering at the end, then return pan to heat and add cabbage, carrot, soy, curry powder, pepper, vinegar and water. Cook, stirring occasionally, for 6 minutes or until cabbage has wilted. Add the noodles and cook for 2 minutes to warm through.

Divide among bowls and top with reserved tofu mixture, crispy fried shallots and more sliced chilli.

use it up
To avoid housing a giant cabbage in your fridge, you could use a pre-cut slaw mix to save even more time. But I have to say this is a fab way to use a ridiculous amount of cabbage.

meat lovers
Sub the tofu for pork mince and throw in some hoisin for a sticky mince sitch.

liquid gold chicken laksa

Is it a soup? Is it noodles? No, it's laska. And yes, I would put it in the same vibe as Superman – actually I'm quite certain Clark Kent ate laksa on the daily. Anyways, cook the laksa. Eat the laksa and be super – cos this is super tasty!

effort 3/5	gluten free	serves 4	prep 10 min	cook 20 min

⅓ cup (100g) laksa paste
1 tbsp tamarind puree
3 garlic cloves
3cm piece ginger
2cm piece fresh turmeric
4 spring onions, white part and
   light green part chopped, green
   part thinly sliced
2 tbsp peanut oil
200g deep-fried tofu*
200g white button mushrooms,
   quartered
2 litres chicken or vegetable stock
400ml can coconut cream
400g chicken tenderloins or breast,
   thinly sliced
200g dried wide rice noodles
juice of 2 limes
2 tbsp fish sauce, plus more if needed
Fresh herbs, crispy fried shallots,
   finely chopped peanuts, bean
   sprouts and chilli paste to serve

Specialty ingredients
Deep-fried tofu can be found in any Chinese grocer but feel free to sub with regular tofu. Though the deep-fried stuff acts like a sponge and soaks up all that laksa goodness to create a gold sponge dripping in flavour – in other words, it's worth finding.

Place laksa paste, tamarind, garlic, ginger, turmeric, and white and light green spring onion in a food processor and whiz until a smooth paste forms.

Heat oil in a large saucepan over medium heat. Add paste and cook, stirring constantly, for 3–4 minutes or until darkened slightly and sticking to the bottom of the pan. Add tofu, mushrooms, stock and coconut cream, stir and bring to the boil. Reduce to a simmer and cook for 15 minutes to reduce slightly. Add chicken and cook gently for a further 5 minutes, or until chicken is cooked through.

Meanwhile cook noodles as per packet instructions, drain and set aside.

Season laksa with lime juice, fish sauce and salt and pepper to taste. Divide noodles among bowls and top with laksa broth, then garnish with sliced green spring onion, fresh herbs, crispy fried shallots, chopped peanuts, bean sprouts and chilli paste to serve.

make it veg — Leave out the chicken and go harder on the tofu for a bowl of veg dreams.

use it up — I'm going to be that annoying person and suggest making your own chicken stock could be really good for this recipe. Veggie trimmings and a leftover roast chook in a pot with lots of water, some peppercorns, aromats; and cook away for 1–2 hours and strain.

TATOR

I'm fully aware you didn't buy this book from the self-help section, but here's some unwarranted life advice I wish I was told at a young age: the secret to life is potato. It's that simple.

SLAP IT TOGETHER

cheesy and chooky loaded fries (pg 82)

GO TO

ultimate potato salad (pg 84)

LONG GAME

twice-cooked garlic lemon potatoes (pg 86)

BAKED FLAKED* MASHED ROASTED BOILED FRIED

*dehydrated potatoes/instant mash

1 Always start with cold water when boiling potatoes. These buttery gems need time to come to terms with the heat and when cooking from cold we allow the starch to ease into becoming soft pillowy tators. A cold start also ensures potatoes are cooked through evenly and perfectly every time.

2 When boiling in a liquid, don't stop at water. While salt is a must, why not take it up a level? Try cooking in stock, throwing in some bay leaves, herbs or even some vinegar for some salt-and-vinegar vibes. By imparting flavour from the get-go, we get to control what flavour direction our tators go in, which can only make for more deliciousness.

3 Embrace the skin. The beauty of potatoes is that by the time we buy them, often they have been washed and prepped to the point where we can just plop them straight into the pot. Put away the peeler, the skin on these guys is delicious and sweet. Plus, there's less fuss required – it's a no brainer.

4 Tators don't need much to be amazing, but a few pieces of equipment could set your mash apart from the rest. Get yourself a ricer for mashed potatoes so as to not overwork the spuds. A mandolin for an ever-so-thin slice that you just can't get with a knife. And a cutting tool like a crinkle cutter is great too for improving the surface area on our potatoes: max area = max goldenness.

5 Use waxy varieties (Nadine, Jersey Benne, Red King Edward, Kipfler, Nicola, Dutch Creams) for anything where you want your potato to stay intact and hold its own when cooked: potato salad, a stewed dish, a curry, or a gratin.

6 Floury potatoes (Russets, Agria, Red Rascal, Coliban) are low in moisture and high in starch, making them good for mash and gnocchi, and good at crisping up for chips.

7 All-rounder tators (Désirée, Rocket, chat, Maris Anchor, purple, Sebago) are semi-starchy and semi-waxy and super versatile. Usually they come washed so I tend to grab for these mostly.

8 Dehydrated potato: I use instant mash a lot. Found near the canned veg at the supermarket, it is a great way of getting starch into things that need binding, and softness, with minimal effort! See my potato gnocchi with amaretti crunch (page 138) to make sense of my madness.

cheesy and chooky loaded fries

Who doesn't love a loaded fry? . . . I imagine anyone who doesn't like soggy Weet-Bix. But for those partial to the sog, this is a total winner! Using up some store-bought or leftover roast chook, these chips are dripping in flavour and gravy. Plates will be licked clean; I can guarantee that.

effort 1/5 · serves 4 as a main, 6–8 as a starter · prep 15 min · cook 40 min

1kg frozen crinkle-cut chips
25g butter
4 spring onions, white part finely chopped, green part thinly sliced
150g mushrooms, thinly sliced
1 tbsp chopped thyme, plus extra sprigs to serve
¼ cup (35g) plain flour
2 cups (300g) shredded store-bought rotisserie chicken
2 cups (500ml) chicken stock
2 tbsp each Worcestershire and soy sauce
100g mozzarella cheese, grated
1 ball fresh buffalo mozzarella, torn into pieces (optional)

Preheat oven to 220ºC fan forced. Line a baking tray with baking paper.

Put chips on prepared tray. Cook for 15–20 minutes, or until golden.

Meanwhile, melt butter in a frypan over medium-high heat. Add white spring onion, mushroom and thyme and cook for 3–4 minutes, or until beginning to turn golden. Add flour and stir to coat in mixture. Cook for 1 minute to cook out slightly.

Add chicken, stock, Worcestershire sauce and soy sauce, and stir to combine. Bring mixture to the boil and cook, stirring regularly, for 5 minutes or until reduced and thickened.

Remove chips from oven and pour over chicken gravy. Scatter with cheeses and return to the top of the oven for 10 minutes, or until bubbling and melted. Serve hot straight from the tray, scattered with spring onions, or divide it up from the tray onto plates.

jazz it up Serve this cheesy goodness with leftover roast veg scattered with bread and butter pickles and dill sprigs to take it up a notch.

make it veg Lose the chicken and stock and sub in porcini powder and veggie stock to make these chips more shroom forward.

ultimate potato salad

This is hands down the best salad to have at or take to a party for a multitude of reasons. Three of them are: 1. It's substantial – so if someone burns the sausages there's at least something you can fill up on; 2. It's already dressed and requires no fuss once you're there; 3. It's delicious (this totally counts as a reason). Don't cheat the recipe, let the onion and pickly things pickle before getting everything mixed together – it's the game changer.

effort 3/5 · gluten free · serves 6–8 as a side · prep 20 min · cook 20 min

1 small red onion, finely chopped
8 cornichons (or any pickle), finely chopped, plus 2 tbsp pickling liquid
finely grated zest and juice of 1 lemon
1kg small clean potatoes, halved
1 tbsp chicken salt
2 bay leaves
8 eggs
150g bacon, chopped
2 tbsp olive oil
1 cup (250g) mayo
1 tbsp wholegrain mustard
½ bunch dill, finely chopped, with some sprigs reserved

Place onion, cornichons, pickling liquid, lemon zest and juice in a bowl and let stand to pickle.

Meanwhile, place potatoes, chicken salt and bay leaves in a saucepan and cover with water. Bring to the boil over medium heat then cook for 10 minutes. Wash eggs then add to saucepan and cook for a further 10 minutes, or until potatoes are cooked through. Drain and transfer potatoes to a large bowl. Cool eggs under a cold tap, then peel and halve.

Place bacon and oil in a frypan over medium-high heat and cook for 4–5 minutes, or until golden and crisp. Combine potatoes, mayo, mustard, eggs and most of the cornichon mixture and dill. Carefully fold to combine then transfer to a serving bowl and top with remaining cornichon mixture, dill and bacon, and serve.

 make it vegan — Lose the bacon, egg chicken salt and mayo and sub in chopped smoked almonds and vegannaise.

m&s with — The T-bone steak with *the* horseradish butter (page 202)

 make it veg — Mixing some sriracha and chilli crisp into the mayo gives this salad a beautiful red colour. Lose the dill and swap in some coriander leaves and finish with crispy fried shallots.

twice-cooked garlic lemon potatoes

The trick with any roast tators is cooking them through in liquid first, then hitting them with fat and dry heat for that crisp crunch we're all striving for. For this recipe I do that all in the one pan by covering it first, then revealing and exposing the tators to soak up the lemon garlic goodness. Delish, and I can confirm it's a good idea to make extra.

effort 2/5	veg	serves 4–6 as a side	prep 15 min	cook 1 hr

1.5kg baby all-rounder potatoes, cleaned
20 garlic cloves, bruised
2 cups (500ml) chicken stock
finely grated zest and juice of 2 lemons
2 tbsp plain flour
2 tbsp extra virgin olive oil
50g butter
a few sprigs oregano , plus extra to serve
100g feta, sliced

Preheat oven to 220°C fan forced.

Place potatoes, garlic, stock and lemon juice in a saucepan and bring to the boil. Transfer to a roasting tray and cover and roast for 40 minutes or until cooked through and most of the liquid has been absorbed.

Remove cover and scatter with flour. Shake in pan to coat and rough up the potato slightly. Add oil, butter, oregano and season with salt and pepper. Cook for a further 20-30 minutes, or until golden.

Scatter over lemon zest, feta and extra oregano sprigs to serve.

make it veg	Ditch the chicken stock and sub for veggie stock and few bay leaves.	spice it up	Chilli flakes are never a bad idea with tators.	m8s with	The leggy roast chook and stuffing, please (page 154). And maybe some broccoli salad with falafel crumb (page 188) as well.

BREAD

My soulmate, my forever, my love. You can't stop me when there's a loaf of fresh bread – be it banana, focaccia, damper, sourdough or sliced white. I play no favourites; I will always say yes to bread.

SLAP IT TOGETHER
baby beer breads
with everything crust
(pg 90)

GO TO
flexi vegan
banana bread
(pg 92)

LONG GAME
cheesy focaccia
(pg 96)

baby beer breads
with everything crust

These breads were born out of lockdown when we all went bananas for baking at home. Losing the need to wait for things to prove and rise, these breads still rise to the challenge – which in this case is to feed me asap. And the everything crust? Well, it's just everything isn't it? Note, once baking this will have your kitchen smelling like your favourite bakery.

 effort 2/5 veg makes 6 prep 5 min cook 45 min

3 cups (450g) plain flour, plus extra
   for dusting
3 tsp baking powder
1 tsp flaky salt
1 tbsp dried mixed herbs
330ml beer (I used a hazy IPA*)
2 tbsp extra virgin olive oil
2 tbsp thick Greek-style yoghurt,
   plus extra for brushing
1 tbsp honey
butter and chives, to serve

Everything spice
2 tbsp sesame seeds, nigella seeds*
linseeds
1 tbsp each garlic granules and
   onion flakes
1 tsp caraway and fennel seeds

Specialty ingredients
Nigella seeds are also known as
onion seeds cos of their onion flavour
– but they aren't actually onion
seeds, confusing right? Regardless,
they can be found in both Indian
and Middle Eastern supermarkets.
Hazy IPA is a super-fruity cloudy
beer I am obsessed with.

Preheat oven to 200°C fan forced. Place a lidded, heavy-based, ovenproof pot in the oven while it heats.

Combine all ingredients for the everything spice in a small bowl.

Combine flour, baking powder, salt and mixed herbs in a large bowl. Add beer, oil, yoghurt and honey and use hands to mix and gently knead to combine.

Lightly flour a clean work surface and tip dough onto it. Divide into 6 and roughly roll into balls. Remove hot pot from the oven and lightly dust with extra flour. Arrange dough balls inside, touching slightly and brush with extra yoghurt to cover, then scatter with 2 tablespoons of the everything spice.

Cover with lid and cook for 45 minutes, or until buns have risen and doubled in size. Remove lid and cook for a further 10 minutes, or until they have a golden crust. Stand to cool in pan.

Slice and serve with lashings of butter, chives (optional) and extra everything spice.

 The sticky harissa glazed salmon (page 162) spooned into these buns with cream cheese and chives – shut your eyes and you can pretty much say it's a bagel.

 Make bulk everything spice and keep in jar to scatter over, well . . . everything.

flexi vegan banana bread

I call this a flexi vegan nani bread cos I myself am not vegan (at this stage) and so I often flex between adding in dairy ingredients and keeping it full vegan. You can't not have this smothered in yoghurt and extra fresh banana slices with a drizzle of syrup. It brings the bread to life if you ask me – just don't expect it to literally dance on your plate.

effort 3/5 · vegan · serves 12 · prep 15 min · cook 1–1¼ hours

650g mashed banana
  (approx. 5–6 ripe bananas)
1½ cups (375g) firmly packed light
  brown sugar
1 cup (250ml) vegetable oil
½ cup (125ml) oat or cows' milk
4 tsp vanilla bean paste
4 tsp ground cinnamon
3¾ cup (550g) self-raising flour
1 cup (100g) rolled oats, plus extra
  for scattering
1 tsp baking powder
yoghurt (plant or cow, depending),
  thinly sliced banana and syrup or
  honey to drizzle

Preheat oven to 160°C fan forced. Grease and line the base and sides of a 30cm x 15m loaf pan with baking paper – alternatively 2 smaller loaf pans 25 x 12cm work also.

Mash bananas in a large bowl and add sugar, oil, milk, vanilla and cinnamon and mix to combine. Add flour, oats and baking powder and mix well to combine.

Transfer to prepared loaf pan, scatter with oats and bake for 1 hour–1¼ hours or until a skewer pierced through the centre comes out clean. Cool in pan for 10 minutes then cool on a wire rack.

Slice and serve toasted and topped with plant or dairy yoghurt, banana and syrup or honey (cos this is flexi after all).

 use it up — Keep overexposed (read: black) bananas in the freezer in 650g clumps so you know you can grab the bag and jump straight into this recipe!

 prep ahead — I like to slice the banana bread and keep slices in the freezer to pop straight into the toaster.

 more veg please — A coarsely grated zucchini or carrot in here, weirdly, is delicious. Just saying.

This dough's been waiting all night for some love! And by that I mean to be folded like a taco and laid down in an oiled tray to PROVE herself and be baked and turned all fluffy . . .

1. The dough has been proving overnight – check them bubbles, a good sign.

2. Bring the dough up from one side.

3. Up, up . . .

7. Cover and leave in a warm place to rise and take shape in the pan.

8. Scatter over cheese.

9. Add tomatoes.

VE IT

. . . your ticket to the land of homemade carbs, turn the page for the recipe with all the measurements you'll need for cooking this Italian stallion.

4. And over, like a taco.

5. Transfer the dough into the oiled baking tray.

6. Prod the dough with fingertips to get the classic focaccia dimples happening.

10. Spike with rosemary.

11. Scatter with salt and pepper and she's ready for the oven.

12. Ta da! Cool in pan for 10 mins, then pull her out and cut with a serrated knife.

cheesy focaccia

There's nothing better than a dough that doesn't require any assistance to be amazing. This bread does exactly that; she's an absolute beauty. Good things take time, great things take more time. But it's safe to say, most of the time needed for this bread is spent with it covered and sitting in the corner of the room like it did something wrong. So don't worry, you're not chained to the stove for this one. And no, it's done nothing but be delicious – and that ain't a crime. See previous page for a step-by-step demo.

effort 4/5 · veg · serves 12 · prep 2 hr · cook 40 min · begin recipe 1 day ahead

2 tsp dried yeast
3 cups (750ml) luke-warm water
1 tbsp honey, plus extra for drizzling
900g (6 cups) strong plain flour*
1 cup (250ml) olive oil, plus extra
   for fingers
3 sprigs rosemary
100g double cream brie, sliced
1 punnet cherry tomatoes, halved

*Specialty ingredient
Strong flour means it's got a higher protein, which is essential for bread making. It can go by various names – high-grade flour, bread flour, even double 00 flour can work for this recipe. It just gives us extra insurance that our bread will rise and be soft.

Dissolve yeast in luke-warm water. Add honey and ¼ cup flour and stand for 10 minutes, or until bubbles form. Add remaining flour and 1 tablespoon of oil. Mix to combine then briefly knead to form a ball.

Cover with a tea towel and set aside in a cool place for 1 hour. Fold like a taco, then spin and fold once more. Cover and leave overnight in a cool place.

The next day, pull and fold the dough. Drizzle a 22cm x 30cm baking tray with ¼ cup oil. Add dough and use oiled fingers to stretch and prod to fill the dish and add indents. Cover and stand in a warm place for 2 hours, or until bubbles form on the surface.

Preheat oven to 220°C fan forced.

Spike dough with rosemary sprigs. Scatter with cheese and tomatoes.

Add a splash of water to the bottom of the oven, to create steam, before baking.

Bake for 35–40 minutes or until the dough has doubled in size, cooked through and golden. Stand to cool slightly. Slice and serve, drizzled with extra olive oil.

---

 make it vegan Lose the cheese and go traditional with tomato and rosemary.

 jazz it up Push sliced cooked potatoes into the dough and top with truffled cheese for something quite close to heaven.

SAM-WICH

Yes, I'm fully aware that I've spelt sandwich wrong. But in case you were unaware, this book was written by someone named Sam Parish (that me) and she is a total fan of a sammy sandwich.

SLAP IT TOGETHER

miso egg fancy sammies (pg 100)

GO TO

ultimate veg sammy (pg 102)

LONG GAME

banh mi with the crispiest pork belly (pg 106)

miso egg fancy sammies

Sometimes a dainty no-crust sandwich is the way to bring the fancy to the party.

(effort 2/5) (veg) (serves 12) (prep 10 min) (cook 10 min)

6 eggs
¼ cup (60g) Kewpie mayo, plus
   2 tbsp extra
1 tbsp red miso paste*
½ tsp shichimi togarashi*, plus
   extra to serve
1 tbsp chopped chives, plus extra
   to serve
juice of ½ lemon
1 loaf white bread
baby herbs, to serve (optional)

*Specialty ingredients
*Miso comes in a variety of forms;
red miso is more full-bodied as it's
aged longer and can contain more
soybeans. In other words, it's got
more flavour. Shichimi togarashi is a
Japanese spice blend of chilli flakes,
sesame seeds and seaweed.*

Bring a medium saucepan of water to the boil. Add eggs and cook for 10 minutes. Drain and rinse under cold water. Peel and mash with a fork and stir in mayo, miso, togarashi, chives and lemon juice. Season to taste.

Spread extra mayo on half of the slices of bread, then place 2 tablespoons of egg mixture in the centre of the other slices. Top egg slices with mayo slices and press edges firmly together to create rounded pockets. Use a serrated knife to cut off crusts.

Halve and serve scattered with baby herbs, or just more chives and togarashi.

jazz it up
I mean these are pretty jazzy, but you could go one step further and serve with mini scones, quiches and a tall glass of bubbles for a real high-tea experience.

use it up
Keep those crusts, pop them into a food processor, and we've got some breadcrumbs for a schnitty (page 208).

ultimate veg sammy

We live for these patties! This is where curry powder truly shows off and takes these vegetable-loaded beauties to another level. And a patty that reaches the edges of the crust?! 'Tis the genius that is a slab patty – thank you, Mr Tray. Double the patties for bulk freezer possibilities. Stored in the freezer, these can be popped into the toaster for the quickest samwich ever.

| effort 3/5 | veg | makes 6 | prep 15 min | cook 25 min |

½ cup (125g) sour cream
12 slices wholemeal bread
2 tomatoes, sliced
6 lettuce leaves
small handful alfalfa sprouts, rinsed
12 slices canned beetroot
1 carrot, coarsely grated
sweet chilli sauce, to serve

Ultimate veg patties
1 small brown onion, finely chopped
   or grated
250g coarsely grated orange
   kūmara/sweet potato
1 tbsp curry powder
400g can lentils, rinsed and drained
1 cup (50g) panko breadcrumbs
2 eggs
2 tbsp vegetable oil

Preheat oven to 220°C fan forced. Grease and line a baking tray with baking paper.

Combine onion, kūmara/sweet potato, curry powder, lentils, panko and eggs in a bowl and season to taste. Transfer to prepared tray and cover with a second sheet of baking paper, then squish down and use a rolling pin to press out so that the slab is 1cm thick. Remove top piece of paper, drizzle with oil and return paper.

Bake for 15 minutes or until cooked through. Remove top piece of paper and cook for a further 5–10 minutes, or until golden. Cut into 6 pieces approx. the size of the bread slices.

Spread sour cream across all bread slices, top with tomato, lettuce, sprouts, beetroot, carrot, and finish with a veg patty, sweet chilli sauce and bread.

Cut and serve.

spice it up
Sub the curry powder for any spice blend that takes your fancy – even a curry paste.

use it up
You can sub in any canned bean or legume with this recipe. Just make sure to give all the ingredients a good mix and squeeze. The patties can be frozen for up to 3 months.

THE ULTIMATE BELLY RUB

This belly rub is just sooo flamin' good! Shame it gets obliterated with a rolling pin to make way for the ULTIMATE pork crackling. Is that really a shame though? No, not at all. Crackle always wins. Turn the page for the recipe and measurements for this belly shake down.

THE CRISPIEST PORK BELLY STEP X STEP

1. Score the skin with a sharp knife or a Stanley knife.

2. Turn over and rub the belly with a marinade, you can go with whatever you like here.

3. Combine the salt and egg whites.

4. Add more salt and egg white as you go to get the snow meringue consistency we're after.

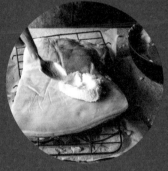

5. Spoon directly onto the skin. More than you think you need so it can form a thick crust.

6. Press out to edges, avoiding the fleshy meat, then roast low and slow.

7. Use a rolling pin or large knife to crack away the salt crust.

8. Crack and discard, brushing away any extra salt on the skin.

9. Blast in a hot oven to crackle. Then rest and slice. Check that crackling!

banh mi
with the crispiest pork belly (aka ultimate belly rub)

Travelling to Vietnam at sixteen with my mum, I got hooked on the flavours of banh mi. This salt-meringue style pork was introduced to me by a friend. It's used a lot in Asian cooking and is the perfect way to ensure the skin on your pork will stay dry and in turn guarantee crisp crackling. Crisp skin pork belly is easy to nail when you have this recipe up your sleeve. It's all about the snow salt that gets baked on top of the skin. It keeps everything dry and when cracked, brushed away and blasted in a hot oven? Well, the results speak for themselves. Check that crackling! I also use this salt mixture for a salt-baked whole fish – it's super versatile. See previous page for a step-by-step demo of the crispy pork belly.

effort	serves	prep	cook
4/5	8	1 hr	1.5 hr

800g whole bone-out pork belly piece
1 piece of lemongrass, finely chopped
1 tbsp olive oil
1 tsp cracked black pepper
1kg table salt
5 egg whites
¼ cup (60ml) fish sauce
2 tbsp soy sauce
2 tsp brown sugar
1 long red chilli, thinly sliced
juice of 1 lime
8 crunchy long rolls or 2 baguettes,
    each cut into 4
¼ cup (50g) your favourite pâté
¼ cup (50g) mayo
½ bunch coriander, sprigs pickled
4 spring onions/shallots, shredded
fridge quickles (page 109) to serve

Preheat oven to 140°C fan forced. Line a baking tray with baking paper and place a rack over the top.

Use a sharp knife or a Stanley knife to score the pork skin. Combine lemongrass, oil and pepper in a bowl. Use to rub the pork meat, avoiding the skin, then place the pork on prepared rack, skin up and exposed. (At this point you can leave the pork overnight to marinate if you have the time.)

Combine salt and egg whites in a bowl until it reaches a snow-like consistency. Use to cover pork skin, avoiding the edges of the belly meat. Roast for 1 hour, or until internal temperature of belly reaches 65°C. Use a rolling pin or large knife to crack off the meringue, and brush with a pastry brush to remove excess salt. Increase oven to 250°C fan forced. Return pork to oven, watching closely for 20–25 minutes until crackling has puffed evenly and completely. Rest for 15 minutes.

Combine fish sauce, soy sauce, sugar, chili and lime juice in a bowl and season to taste.

Carve belly and spoon over sauce to season.

To assemble rolls, spread pâté and mayo inside roll and fill with coriander, shredded spring onion and fridge quickles. Add pork and drizzle over any extra sauce.

jazz it up	Serve in bao buns with hoisin and shredded spring onions/shallots for something a little fancy.	use it up	Use the glaze from gochujang-glazed eggplant (page 194) and brush over crispy pork then finish on the grill for a whole other layer of flavour.

FLAVOUR ME

Staring into the pantry or fridge trying to get some inspiration??
Sometimes food just needs another layer of yumbles, a new lick of flavour
to keep the interest thriving. For this we need flavour-packed ingredients
that do a lot of the work for us. So here is some condiment inspiration to
keep you enthused when cooking something for the upteenth time, or
trying to give some leftovers a rebrand. For loads more information, head
to the front of the book for extra ingredient details.

CREAMY

Whole-egg mayo
Kewpie mayo
Flavoured mayo
French onion dip (page 30)
Hummus (page 32)
Buttermilk dressing (page 176)

SPICY

Hot sauce
Date and tamarind chutney
Chilli crisp
Mango chutney
Eggplant chutney
Mustard – Dijon, American,
wholegrain
Za'atar
Dukkah

When in doubt,
a squeeze of
lemon, flaky salt and
cracked pepper and
a good drizz of olive
oil is always a good
idea!

PICKLED/ FERMENTED

Dill pickles
Kimchi
Pickled jalapeños
Pickled ginger
Sauerkraut
Cornichons
Canned beetroot
Fridge quickles

SAUCY

Smoky BBQ sauce
Tomato sauce
Sriracha
Onion and tomato relish
Pesto (page 132)
Soy sauce
Kecap manis

Fridge quickles

Cut **1 carrot** and **1 daikon** into 1cm batons. Quarter **1 bunch of radishes**. Place vegetables in separate jars. Place **1 cup (250ml) rice wine vinegar**, **½ cup (110g) caster sugar** and **1½ cups (375ml) water** in a saucepan. Add spices: I used **3 makrut lime leaves** and **1 star anise**, but you could use coriander seeds, peppercorns, dill, caraway – the options are endless. Place saucepan over medium-high heat and cook, stirring until sugar dissolves. Bring mixture to the boil then remove from heat

and pour over vegetables and stand to cool. Use straight away and/or secure with a lid and place in the fridge until ready to use. These will keep in the fridge for up to 4 months.

These fridge quickles and the pickling liquid can be kept in the fridge and added to with any scraps you have like cucumber or onions. Keeping in the fridge means you can't keep them as long as fully pickled veggies but it does a good job of extending their life.

110 WRAP ME

WRAP ME

I love a wrap – it's a skinnier version of bread that can hold liquid just that little bit better. Safe to say there will still be sauce running down my wrist with these recipes. And that's a wrap.

SLAP IT TOGETHER

3-cheese crêpes with cheat's béchamel (pg 112)

GO TO

pork larb in roti (pg 114)

LONG GAME

mincey burritos with cheesy rice and beans (pg 116)

3-cheese crêpes
with cheat's béchamel

Brunch goals are on point here. This cheat's béchamel is a game changer for toasties, lasagne – anything that needs a melty oozy sauce without the hassle of a roux. That's not to say I'm not a fan of a roux (flour and butter); it has its place. Regardless of all this roux chat, these crêpes are scrummy. It should be said that because this is slap it together, I've gone for store-bought crêpes, but there's a recipe at the bottom of the page if you've got time to make your own.

effort 1/5   serves 4   prep 10 min   cook 20 min

8 store-bought crêpes
8 slices raclette or Tasty cheese, halved
8 slices shaved-off-the-bone leg ham
8 button mushrooms, thinly sliced
2 tomatoes, chopped
2 tbsp finely grated Parmesan
chopped chives to serve

Cheat's béchamel
⅔ cup (150g) sour cream
1½ cups (150g) shredded mozzarella
½ tsp each ground nutmeg and onion powder
¼ tsp ground clove
2 tbsp finely grated Parmesan

Preheat oven to 200ºC fan forced. Grease and line a baking tray with baking paper.

For the cheat's béchamel, combine all ingredients and season to taste.

Divide béchamel among crêpes then top with cheese, ham, mushroom and tomato. Season with salt and pepper. Roll up, then transfer to prepared tray. Cover in foil and bake for 10 minutes, or until cheese is melted. Remove foil, scatter with Parmesan and bake for a further 5–10 minutes, or until golden.

Scatter with chives and serve.

jazz it up

Feeling like some homemade crêpes? 1 cup each milk and plain flour + 1 egg, whizzed in a jug with a stick blender then left to rest for 5 minutes. Use ¼ cup measurement to pour into a hot oil-sprayed frypan and cook, one side only, for 2–3 minutes or until just cooked through. Repeat x 8.

use it up

Any cheese can go in here. Use up end bits in the cheat's béchamel and crumble anything else into the filling. You could also use tortillas in place of the crêpes, if you have some you need to use up.

pork larb in roti

Talk about a party in your mouth! Larb has always been a fave for me, but partnered with my favourite flat bread, a good amount of fresh herbs, a good schmear of hoisin and some pork crackle to finish things off . . . well, I could call this one of my favourite bites of food in this book. Feel free to sub in crumbled tofu, chicken, turkey or beef mince or even some firm white fish. It's an everything sort of recipe; all proteins allowed.

effort 3/5 · serves 4–6 · prep 15 min · cook 10 min

4–6 store-bought fresh or frozen roti*
400g pork mince
1 bunch coriander, leaves picked, stems and root finely chopped
1 tbsp sambal oelek*
2 tbsp hoisin, plus extra to serve
2 tbsp coconut or vegetable oil
1 red onion, thinly sliced
1 long red chilli, thinly sliced, plus extra to serve
2 tbsp fish sauce
finely grated zest and juice of 2 limes
1 telegraph cucumber, outside peeled into ribbons, inner core cut into chunks
1 lettuce, leaves separated
1 carrot, shredded
pork crackle*, mint, and Thai basil leaves, to serve

*Specialty ingredients
Roti can come fresh or frozen. It's a beautiful buttery flat bread that is perfect for wrapping and dipping into things. Here I've used an Indian version, but the Thai version can be even more flaky if that's more your thing. Sambal oelek is a chili sauce found in most Asian grocers and some supermarkets. Pork crackle is found in the snacks section of your supermarket, usually near the nuts, and is a great one to have on hand for adding crunchiness.

Prepare roti as per packet instructions to warm through.

Combine pork mince, coriander stems and root, sambal and hoisin in a bowl.

Heat oil in a frypan over medium heat. Add mince mixture and cook, stirring and breaking apart with a wooden spoon, for 6–8 minutes, or until cooked through and beginning to stick to the bottom of the pan. Remove from heat and stir through onion, chilli, fish sauce, lime juice and zest. Stand for 5 minutes to pickle slightly. Season to taste then stir through the cucumber chunks.

Spoon extra hoisin across roti. Top with lettuce and spoon over mince. Top with cucumber ribbons, carrot, pork crackle and herbs and extra fresh chilli slices.

---

jazz it up
Use the dough in pesto margi pan pizza (page 222) to make your own flat breads – roll out to 5mm thin and cook for 4–5 minutes on each side in a frypan.

more veg please
Ditch the carbs and serve these wrapped in the lettuce leaves with some shredded green mango or papaya.

mincey burritos
with cheesy rice and beans

Something like these mincey burritos are sure to have graced your table during your childhood. Easy pan sauce, salad things on the table and boom, dinner is served. My mincey burritos get spiced with cocoa for some mole vibes and come with a side of cheesy rice to fill out the tortilla. Also, my super-fast salsa brings some heat to these wraps and makes for some tasty leftovers.

 effort 4/5 serves 4–6 prep 20 min cook 30 min

2 tbsp olive oil
1 brown onion, finely chopped
1 bunch coriander, leaves picked, stems finely chopped
3 garlic cloves, 2 of them finely chopped
400g beef or pork mince
400g can kidney beans, rinsed and drained
2 tsp each ground cumin, smoked paprika, oregano
1 tsp cocoa powder
¼ cup (70g) tomato paste
1 cup (250ml) water
2 tomatoes, chopped
¼ cup (30g) pickled jalapeños, plus 2 tbsp pickling liquid
sour cream, sliced tomatoes, lettuce and tortillas, to serve

Cheesy rice and beans
1½ cups (300g) long grain rice
1 chicken stock cube, crumbled
2 cups (500ml) water
400g can black beans, rinsed and drained
100g grated Tasty cheese
2 garlic cloves, finely grated

Heat oil in a frypan over medium heat. Add onion and coriander stems and cook, stirring, for 3–4 minutes, or until softened. Add chopped garlic and mince and cook, breaking up with a wooden spoon, for 5 minutes, or until browned off. Add beans, spices, cocoa and tomato paste and cook, stirring and mashing beans slightly, for 2 minutes, or until aromatic. Add water and reduce heat and cook for 10 minutes, or until meat is tender. Season to taste.

Meanwhile, for the rice, place rice, stock cube and water in a saucepan over high heat. Bring to the boil then cover and reduce heat to low. Cook for 12 minutes, or until cooked through. Add beans and cheese and stand covered to warm through for 5 minutes. Add garlic and stir through with a fork to fluff rice and disperse garlic, beans and cheese.

To make the salsa, whiz tomato, jalapeño, pickling liquid, remaining whole garlic and half the coriander leaves in a small food processor. Season to taste.

Serve mince, rice and beans, salsa, sour cream, sliced tomato, lettuce, remaining coriander leaves and tortillas and assemble at the table.

 make it veg Lose the mince and up the beans with a handful of mushrooms. Also, guac to finish, which is a good idea however you have it.

 use it up Leftover salsa can be kept in the fridge in a sealed container for up to 4 weeks. Also, it's never a bad idea to make extra mince and freeze it. Cram it into tortillas and into a lined baking dish with a bottle of passata and cheese and you got yourself some enchiladas.

LONG PASTA

Twirling, coiling, twisting, turning pasta. These forked, bended and curled spoonfuls have never-ending possibilities. Yes, that was essentially a poem about pasta that you probably didn't realise you needed until now. You're welcome. Also, expect some Bolognese in here, the ultimate dinner table convo starter: 'What's your secret ingredient?'

SLAP IT TOGETHER

chilli lemon
prawn linguine
(pg 120)

GO TO

cauli
carbonara
(pg 122)

LONG GAME

sam's secret-ingredients
bolognese
(pg 126)

chilli lemon prawn linguine

Seafood marinara was trending in my fam meals growing up. Fast forward to being an adult and it seems almost like a light-bulb moment as to how easy and quick seafood is on a weeknight. Get ready to be transported to the coastline of the Mediterranean. And, SHOCKER! I'm not against a bit of Parmesan here — it's not a culinary crime to pair it with seafood if you ask me.

effort 2/5 · serves 4 · prep 10 min · cook 15 min

⅓ cup (80ml) olive oil
5 garlic cloves, thinly sliced
1 bunch parsley, stems finely sliced, leaves picked and finely chopped
1 long red chilli, thinly sliced (seeds removed if you're not a fan of too much heat)
½–1 tsp chilli flakes (depending on how hot you like it)
1 tsp crushed fennel seeds
1 punnet cherry tomatoes
750g good quality prawn meat
juice of 1 lemon, plus wedges to serve
400g store-bought fresh linguine
2 tbsp chopped capers

Bring a large saucepan of water to the boil.

Heat oil in a deep-sided frypan over medium heat, add garlic, parsley stems, chilli and fennel seeds and cook, stirring, for 2–3 minutes, or until garlic is golden. Add tomatoes and prawns and cook, stirring and tossing, for 4 minutes or until prawns are just cooked through. Add lemon juice, and parsley leaves and remove from heat.

Add pasta to the boiled water and cook for 1–2 minutes, or until it begins to float to the surface. Use long tongs to transfer pasta to pan with prawns. Add half a cup pasta-cooking water to pan and return to high heat, adding more pasta water as needed. Stir to coat and season to taste.

Transfer to bowls and scatter with capers, grind over black pepper, and serve immediately with extra lemon wedges alongside.

jazz it up

Feel like taking this up a notch? How about making your own pasta? I'm a fan of a pasta recipe with a touch of tomato paste for colour. My go-to dough is 100g flour + 1 egg + 1 tsp tomato paste per person. Mixxy mixxy, resty resty, rolly rolly (by hand even), slicey, slicey and cook until it floats. BOOM!

spice it up

Flip the spice and lose the chilli, subbing in some thinly sliced fennel or some ice-cube pesto (page 132) for a punch of fresh.

cauli carbonara

I almost called this pasta ala' bacon and eggs but 'cauli carb' has a good ring to it. Enjoyed with friends and tall glasses of wine, this is comfort food at its finest!

effort 2/5 · serves 4 · prep 10 min · cook 15 min

300g dried mafaldine pasta* or any long-style pasta

1 cauliflower, core removed and finely chopped, florets broken into small pieces (keep separate)

25g butter

200g bacon or speck, chopped into batons

1 leek, white part only, thinly sliced

2 tsp cracked pepper

1 sprig rosemary, plus extra to serve

4 garlic cloves, thinly sliced

3 egg yolks

80g freshly grated Parmesan (must be FRESH)

Specialty ingredient
Mafaldine pasta – a ribbon-shaped pasta with wavy edges to catch saucy thangs. It's perfect for a carbonara, but easily substituted with your fave long pasta.

Bring a large pot of water to the boil. Add pasta and cauliflower florets and cook as per pasta packet instructions. (Try to get a pasta that takes at least 7 minutes, so the cauliflower is cooked through, otherwise add it earlier.)

Meanwhile place butter, bacon, leek, pepper, rosemary and cauliflower core in a large frypan over medium-high heat and cook for 5–6 minutes, or until beginning to turn golden. Stir through garlic and cook for 1 minute, or until aromatic. Stand until required.

Strain pasta and cauliflower, reserving 2 cups pasta water, and add to frypan along with egg yolks, Parmesan and 1 cup of pasta water. Stir well to combine and coat. Return to low heat and cook, stirring for 1 minute to warm through and coat pasta. Add more pasta water depending on how saucy you like it. Scatter extra rosemary and serve hawt.

jazz it up

Obvious, but some chilli flakes in here can really crank the heat, or sub in any kind of hard herb you fancy – thyme, oregano or some marjoram works well.

more veg please

If you're dying for some more veg with this dish, a cup of frozen peas, corn or even some fresh or frozen spinach thrown in the mix should sort it out.

SAUCY SECRETS

From favourite child to least (which really means I love them all and can't choose), here are the 10 secret ingredients for my Bolognese sauce (page 126) . . .

1. THE HOLY TRINITY + THE FORGOTTEN ONE:

Aka onion, carrot, celery and parsley stems. Look, I totally understand if the celery gets cut, cos who wants to buy a giant celery for one stick of the stuff, but that's where the forgotten one, parsley, comes into play. The stems do a great job of mimicking the flavours of celery. Carrot and onion are a non-negotiable though. Onion for savoury vibes, carrot for sweetness.

2. COMBO MINCE

Whether it's pork and beef, veal and pork or lamb and beef. You want something fatty and something more lean to carry the heft.

3. LOTS OF CANNED TOMATOES

Diced or whole tomatoes, but I do prefer whole cos it has taken one less process to get to you. Don't be shy with the tomatoes! Also should be said if you don't have 10,000 of these in your pantry, who even are you?

4. GARLIC

Yes, 6 garlic cloves because I swear garlic just isn't as punchy anymore. Pretty obvious why garlic is important. It's garlic.

5. EXTRA VIRGIN OLIVE OIL

This sounds like a lot of olive oil, but extra virgin is essentially olive juice so it's okay by me, and it does a great job of buddying everything together flavour-wise.

6. MILK

Because it knows how to tone down the temper of a tomato and get the sauce hella silky. I'm still shocked more people aren't putting this in their Bolognese.

7. A LITTLE NUTMEG AND CINNAMON

The nutmeg gives savoury tones; the cinnamon sweet. Together they are unstoppable and help this meaty sauce carry itself with flair and poise.

8. PARMESAN RIND

This is a condensed almost fossil-like food, a source of pure cheesy goodness we should all be making better use of! It's totally fine if you don't have a Parmesan rind; it won't be lost without it, but if you're not buying Parm wedges, please consider it. An investment in flavour I truly think you should be getting on board with. Keep all the rinds in the freezer for exactly this.

9. ANCHOVIES

Anchovies are totes optional, but they do add a great depth of flavour, sometimes a little sea helps ground a dish . . . makes sense, right?

10. BAY LEAVES AND RED RED WINE

These are less important I guess. But I also would be sad if they weren't included.

sam's secret-ingredients bolognese

Watching Dad make Bolognese growing up, I always tried to pin down what the secret ingredient was, and when I started making my own (at like, 12 years old, can I add), I started introducing my own 'secret ingredients' like brown sugar and BBQ sauce — little did I know half the secret was giving it time to really settle in and cook away to gain sweetness from the carrot. But yes, my current (cos I'm sure it will change again by next year) recipe has many secret ingredients we should all be throwing in!

effort 3/5 | serves 4 with plenty of leftover sauce | prep 30 min | cook 2.5 hr

1 brown onion, chopped
1 carrot, chopped
1–2 sticks celery, chopped
½ bunch any kind of parsley, leaves picked and finely chopped, stems reserved
few sprigs each thyme and/or oregano
⅓ cup (80ml) extra virgin olive oil
½ tsp each ground nutmeg and cinnamon
3 anchovies
250g beef mince
250g pork mince
⅓ cup (80ml) red wine (I went for a Syrah for this, but whatever you're drinking, this bol will love)
2 tbsp tomato paste
6 garlic cloves, finely chopped
4 x 400g cans diced or whole tomatoes
2 cups (500ml) milk
2 bay leaves
30g freshly grated Parmesan, rind reserved
400g dried spaghetti
garlic bread, to serve

Whiz onion, carrot, celery (the holy trinity), parsley stems, thyme and oregano in a food processor, scraping down the sides halfway, until finely chopped.

Heat oil in a heavy-based saucepan over medium-low heat. Add veg and spices and cook, stirring frequently, for 8–10 minutes or until softened and beginning to caramelise — usually it's getting there when you can see the oils again after the veg has absorbed them. Increase heat to high and add anchovies and minces. Use a wooden spoon to mix and break up the mince then cook, stirring, for 4–5 minutes, or until mince is browned all over.

Add wine, tomato paste and garlic and cook for 3 minutes, or until aromatic and most of the wine has been absorbed. Add tomatoes and a can-full (350ml) of water — use the same water to rinse out each can to get all the tomato goodness out. Bring to the boil, then add milk, bay leaves and Parmesan rind.

Return to a gentle simmer then cook over low heat for 2 hours, or until reduced and delicious — or if you're like me, transfer to a slow cooker so you don't have to think about it (high for 4 hours or low for 8 is good). Season with salt and pepper to taste.

To serve, cook pasta as per packet instructions. Add to a clean saucepan and ladle over as much sauce as you like, return to heat and shimmy with tongs to coat the long strands of pasta. Transfer remaining sauce to a container for never-ending meal options. (Did I hear lasagne?)

Divide among bowls, scatter with Parmesan, chopped parsley and serve with garlic bread.

jazz it up — Layer into a lasagne or toss through cooked rigatoni and bake with cheese for a prima donna pasta bake.

spice it up — A good hit of some Mexican spices, chilli and a few cans of beans and this turns into the ultimate chilli con carne. Serve with rice and sour cream.

SHORT PASTA

Ambitious beings destined for sauce and willing to take on whatever you throw at them — yes, I'm still talking about short pasta. I'm a tad obsessed; and I'll take them any shape they come.

SLAP IT TOGETHER
ice-cube pesto pasta (pg 132)

GO TO
one-pot penne (pg 134)

LONG GAME
potato and sage gnocchi with amaretti crunch (pg 138)

ICE ICE, BABY

Alright STOP pesto and listen; Sam is back with a brand new invention. Something grabs hold of my ice cube tray tightly. Flows in green daily and nightly. Will I ever stop? Well, I'd say no — put me in the freezer and I'll glow. Dun dun dun da da dun dun. Ice ice, baby! Turn the page for the recipe. Close the book for a mic drop.

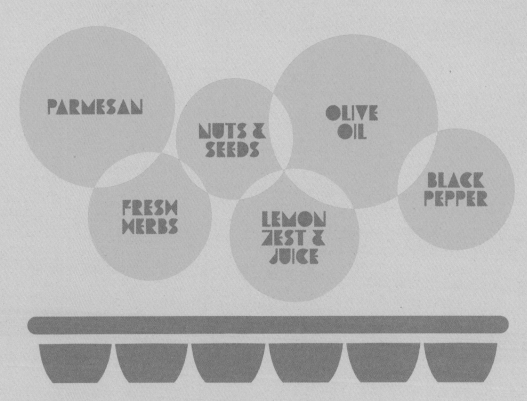

PARMESAN

NUTS & SEEDS

OLIVE OIL

BLACK PEPPER

FRESH HERBS

LEMON ZEST & JUICE

ICE-CUBE PESTO STEP X STEP

1. Whiz the Parmesan or pecorino.

2. Add the nuts/seeds.

3. Add the herbs.

4. Add lemon zest and juice, garlic and pepper.

5. Add olive oil.

6. Whiz until it gets super green and warm to touch.

7. Pour into trays.

8. Flatten top to distribute evenly, then pop in the freezer.

9. Pop out! Trust me, the bright green returns when it hits the heat.

ice-cube pesto pasta

The best kind of tasty, ice-cube pesto is the ultimate freezer hack. I grab lots of shapes of ice cube trays at the second-hand stores especially for these sorts of things, so keep an eye out! There's nothing more satisfying than pouring this green deliciousness into a crisp white ice cube tray. I like to keep a spoon back for myself. After freezing, pop out the portioned cubes to be stored back in the freezer for the quickest dinner ever. Its freshness is locked in and you will be elated with happiness. I used a mixture of greens, but if you want full traditional, go all-out basil. Here it's paired with pasta mista and baby spinach.
See previous page for a step-by-step demo of the ice-cube pesto.

effort 2/5 · veg · serves 4 · prep 10 min · cook 10 min

400g pasta mista*, or any short
  pasta you like
100g baby spinach leaves
finely grated Parmesan, to serve

Ice-cube pesto (makes 400g)
100g assorted nuts/seeds (I used
  walnuts, almonds, cashews and
  pine nuts)
1 tsp cracked black pepper
100g hard cheese (I used both
  pecorino and Parmesan, as I store
  leftover bits in the freezer)
100g green leaves (I used basil,
  parsley, coriander and baby spinach)
100ml extra virgin olive oil
finely grated zest and juice of
  2 lemons (100ml juice)
5 garlic cloves, chopped

Specialty ingredient
*Mista is Italian for mixed. Pasta mista
is a packet of lots of different shapes.*

To make the pesto, microwave the nuts/seeds and pepper 2–3 times in 20-second intervals, until aromatic and slightly golden. (Alternatively, toast in the oven, but the microwave is way easier.)

Place cheese in a blender and whiz until finely chopped. Add remaining ingredients and whiz, scraping down the sides and stirring regularly, for 3 minutes, or until warm to touch and smooth and green (the mix will stay green if it gets a bit warm).

Use fresh, or transfer to an ice tray and place in the freezer. The next day, pop out pesto cubes and transfer to an airtight container or bag. The pesto cubes will keep in the freezer for up to 3 months.

Cook pasta as per packet instructions. Drain, reserving 1 cup of the pasta water. Return water to saucepan along with 4–6 cubes (100g) of pesto and stir until melted and combined. Return pasta to pan along with baby spinach and stir through to coat in pesto. Cook for 1–2 minutes to warm through. Serve scattered with extra Parmesan.

spice it up Ditch the nuts and Parmesan, sub the green things for coriander, mint and spinach and add 2 long green chillis, 1 tsp chaat masala and a 2cm piece of ginger and you got yourself your own coriander/mint chutney in ice-cube form.

more veg please Halved cherry tomatoes or adding some zucchini noodles to the mix is sure to hit the veggie goals.

one-pot penne

A painless plate of penne pasta – say that fast six times, and by the time you nail that I reckon this plate of painless penne pasta will be ready to eat! This is one of my all-time fave dishes. If I had TikTok (and who knows maybe I do by now), I'd say it would go viral – mainly because the pasta gets cooked in the sauce; I don't kid about one pot, it's not to be underestimated!

| effort 2/5 | serves 6 | prep 5 min | cook 25 min |

6 fresh sausages (I went with an
 Italian-style, which is usually a
 pork and beef sausage flavoured
 with herbs and fennel seeds)
⅓ cup (80ml) extra virgin olive oil
1 long red chilli, thinly sliced
5 garlic cloves, thinly sliced
6 anchovies, finely chopped (make
 it pasty)
handful basil leaves, plus extra
 to serve
¼ cup (60ml) white wine
500g penne pasta (check the packet
 and opt for a penne with a 10 min
 cooking time)
3 x 400g cans cherry tomatoes
finely grated fresh Parmesan, to serve

Slit sausage casings and squeeze out filling onto a plate and create roughly 2cm meatballs. If you're as immature as me, this can be awkward – sorry in advance.

Heat oil in a large saucepan over high heat. Add chilli, garlic and anchovy and cook for 3–5 minutes, or until it reaches the golden zone and smells aromatic. Add basil leaves and sausage meatballs and cook, stirring reasonably carefully for 4–5 minutes, or until cooked through. Add wine and bring to the boil, stirring, to deglaze the pan.

Add pasta and cook for 1–2 minutes, or until shiny and warmed through. Add cherry tomatoes, then refill cans with water and add to pan (approx. 1.2 litres). Season with salt and pepper, stir to combine, then bring to the boil. Cook with lid off, stirring frequently (super important to prevent stickage-freakage) for 9 minutes (1 minute less than what the pasta packet says) or until pasta is cooked through.

Divide among bowls and scatter with Parmesan, basil leaves and cracked pepper to serve.

| make it veg | Lose the sausage and anchovies and go veggie all the way. | use it up | Any canned tomatoes work in this one if you're trying to get rid of the tower of tomatoes in the back of your pantry. |

GNOCCH GNOCCH

Who's there? Wooooooo. Wooooooooo who? Glad you're excited about this cheat gnocchi recipe too! Yes your eyes don't deceive you there are no round-looking potatoes in these shots . . . You'll just have to turn the page for the full recipe to figure out why.

POTATO GNOCCHI STEP X STEP

1. Combine dehydrated potato and boiling water in a large bowl.

2. Mix to combine.

3. Add egg, nutmeg and a pinch of salt and pepper.

4. Mix to combine.

5. Add flour and incorporate into dough gently until it forms a ball.

6. Once semi-incorporated, start using your hands to bring it together and briefly knead.

7. Cut into 4 pieces.

8. Roll each piece into a 2cm thick sausage.

9. Transfer to a piece of baking paper and cut into 2cm pieces.

10. Use the back of a fork to press and roll the gnocchi over and create grooves; this helps grab more sauce.

11. Continue with remaining dough.

12. Dust with extra flour and use paper to transfer to cook in boiling water.

potato gnocchi
with herby garlic butter and amaretti crunch

This recipe was born from a family of campers that love good food. My mum's famous gnocchi was invented while camping. No, we are not Italian, but based on how we eat we might as well be. The dehydrated potato was a genius play by my mum plucked from the wisdom of a Melbourne chef, so I reckon it's been given the all clear in terms of being allowed. It truly makes gnocchi at home so simple! The easiest gnocchi that ever lived, and the softest too. And the amaretti biscuits for crunch? Well you'll just have to trust me on that one! *See previous page for a step-by-step demo of making gnocchi.*

| effort 3/5 | veg | serves 4 | prep 20 min | cook 10 min |

120g garlic butter
1 bunch oregano or sage,
   sprigs picked
juice of 1 lemon
50g amaretti biscuits*
shaved Manchego* (sub with
   Parmesan or Grana Padano)
   to serve
baby basil leaves, to serve

Cheat's gnocchi
2 cups (100g) dehydrated
   potato flakes*
1 cup (250ml) of boiling water
1 egg
½ cup (75g) plain flour, plus
   extra for dusting

Specialty ingredients
Amaretti biscuits and Manchego cheese are found in most delis and Italian grocers. Dehydrated potato flakes/instant mash can be found in all supermarkets, usually near the canned veg. Just check the ingredients list; it should be 100% dehydrated potato and nothing else.

To make the cheat's gnocchi, combine dehydrated potato and boiling water in a large bowl and mix to combine. Stand to cool slightly. Add egg and a pinch of salt and pepper and mix to combine – I like to use my hands to do this. Add flour and incorporate into dough gently until it forms a ball, working the dough like you would a scone dough. The mixture might seem dry at first but with each fold it should come together.

Divide into 4 pieces, then roll each piece into a 2cm-thick sausage. Transfer to a piece of baking paper and cut into 2cm pieces. Use a fork to push down and roll on each piece – this adds to the surface area, creating grooves which helps grab more sauce (read: flavour). Bring a large saucepan of salted water to the boil.

Meanwhile, place butter and herbs in a saucepan over medium-high heat. Melt then cook for 3–4 minutes until foam subsides and you're left with light brown butter and crisp leaves. Stir through lemon juice and season to taste.

Use the baking paper to lift gnocchi and add to boiling water.

Cook for 1–2 minutes, or until gnocchi float to the surface. Remove with a slotted spoon and add to prepared sauce. Cook sauce and gnocchi over high heat for 1 minute or until warmed through.

Divide gnocchi among serving bowls and scatter with amaretti, shaved Manchego and baby basil leaves to serve.

use it up — Any herbs can be thrown in to flavour the butter. Leftover roast spuds? Mash them up and throw into the gnocchi dough!

prep ahead — Make the dough and chill, to be used within 4–5 hours.

RICE

When you're craving a bowl of warm nourishing rice with all the trimmings, these recipes have you covered with spice, flavour and richness. A global selection from Indonesia to Egypt to Italy, rice is a demonstration of the thing I love most about food – it connects us and teaches us to be open minded as there are thousands of ways a grain of rice can reach the table. How can you not find hope in that?

SLAP IT TOGETHER

chilli basil coconut
fried rice
(pg 142)

GO TO

koshari
(pg 144)

LONG GAME

mushroom and
black garlic risotto
(pg 146)

chilli basil coconut fried rice

This rice dish is the most forkable plate of food – meaning it's hard to take a breath between mouthfuls. Indonesian cuisine has this incredible talent of only writing smash hits and hitting all the killer notes for a number one on the charts every single time. Yes, I just related food to music hits and I am so okay with that. I would happily have this every night of the week.

effort 3/5	gluten free	serves 4	prep 10 min	cook 20 min

2 cups (400g) jasmine rice
400ml coconut milk
1 pandan leaf*, tied in a knot (optional)
1 cup (250ml) water
¼ cup (60ml) vegetable oil
2 tbsp dried anchovies*, chopped
¼ cup (35g) raw peanuts
2 French shallots, finely chopped
   (can sub with 1 small brown onion)
2 garlic cloves, thinly sliced
6 fresh shiitake mushrooms, thinly sliced
4 eggs
¼ cup (75g) sambal oelek, plus extra
   to serve
2 tbsp kecap manis*, plus extra to serve
½ bunch basil (or holy basil, if you can
   get your hands on it)
sliced cucumber and tomato, to serve

*Specialty ingredient
Pandan leaves are from the tropical pandanus plant, and are used in Southeast and South Asian cuisine – these fragrant leaves can be found fresh if you're lucky or typically frozen in Asian supermarkets. Dried anchovies are found in Asian supermarkets with the other dried fish. They can be a little confronting to look at but give an incredible depth to this rice dish. Grab the kecap manis (a sweet soy sauce) while you're there.

Place rice, coconut milk, pandan leaf (if using) and water in a wok over high heat. Bring to the boil then reduce heat to low. Cover and cook for 12 minutes, or until rice is cooked through. Fluff with a fork and transfer to a tray to cool slightly.

Clean pan and return to high heat with 2 tablespoons oil. Add anchovies and peanuts and cook for 1–2 minutes, or until turning golden. Add French shallot, garlic and mushroom and cook, stirring, for 3 minutes or until softened. Transfer to tray with rice.

Return wok to heat with remaining oil. Crack eggs into a bowl and whisk with 2 tablespoons water. Add to wok, swirling to coat the surface and create a thin omelette. Bring edges in then swirl again and cook, without touching, for 1–2 minutes, or until cooked through. Roughly cut with a spoon then add rice and veg mixture, sambal, kecap manis and most of the basil and cook, stirring, for 3 minutes, or until coated and cooked through.

Divide among serving bowls and serve with cucumber and tomato, extra sambal and kecap manis to serve.

jazz it up
Boil eggs for 10 minutes. Refresh in iced water, peel and transfer to a bowl with 1 tsp turmeric, 2 tbsp soy sauce and 1 tbsp rice vinegar. Toss to coat and chill overnight to marinate and pickle slightly. Halve and serve with rice and ditch the omelette element of the dish.

use it up
Make double coconut rice and use some straight away with a curry, chill the remaining and use it to make this dish the next day.

koshari

This was one of the first things we ate when we travelled to Egypt on our honeymoon. We'd somehow been talked into buying some artwork, and I'd mentioned I wanted to try koshari. Before I knew it, a delivery arrived and two minutes later, I was spooning the koshari into my starving, jet-lagged mouth. Delicious doesn't seem big enough a word. This is my simplified version for a quick mid-week feed!

| effort 2/5 | veg | serves 4 | prep 10 min | cook 20 min |

1 large brown onion, thinly sliced
1 tsp flaky salt
⅓ cup (80ml) extra virgin olive oil, divided
¼ cup (45g) golden vermicelli* (sub with small macaroni)
2 tbsp dried puy lentils
1 cup (200g) long-grain rice
2 cups (500ml) cold water
400g can chickpeas, rinsed and drained
2 garlic cloves, finely chopped
1 tbsp baharat* or ras-el-hanout*
1 tsp chilli flakes
400g can chopped tomatoes
1 tbsp pomegranate molasses* (can sub with 1 tsp each sugar and white vinegar)
coriander leaves, shredded, to serve

*Specialty ingredients
Golden vermicelli pasta is a wheat-based dried noodle. Baharat and ras-el-hanout are both spice blends and pomegranate molasses is a sweet and sour syrup – all found in Middle Eastern grocers.

Toss onion and salt in a bowl and stand to soften.

Meanwhile, heat 1 tablespoon oil in a saucepan over high heat. Add noodles and lentils and cook for 1–2 minutes or until warmed through and noodles are golden. Add rice and stir to coat in oil then add water and bring to the boil. Reduce heat to low, cover and cook for 12 minutes, or until rice, noodles and lentils are cooked through. Add chickpeas and stir to coat. Cover and stand for 5 minutes.

Heat remaining oil in a frypan over high heat. Add salted onions and cook for 4 minutes, or until browned, crisp and beginning to burn – but not burnt (I know, so technical). Remove with a slotted spoon, return oil to heat with garlic and spices and cook for 1 minute, or until aromatic. Add tomatoes and molasses and bring to the boil. Cook for 5 minutes, or until reduced by half.

Divide rice mixture among serving bowls and top with tomato mixture, crispy onions and shredded coriander.

| use it up | Up the chilli in the sauce – the rice mixture can take some heat. | prep ahead | The tomato sauce can be made in advance and kept in a jar in the fridge so it's a quick case of cooking the rice and reheating sauce. |

mushroom and black garlic risotto

The meatiness of mushrooms is fully apparent in this plate of risotto. The black garlic in here mirrors the shrooms in flavour and brings another level of depth to the rice. Finished with some finely grated pecorino and truffle oil, cos why not. This is one special plate of risotto – so special I imagine you'll be heading back for thirds.

effort 3/5	veg	gluten free	serves 4	prep 15 min	cook 30 min

1 vegetable stock cube
20g dried porcini mushrooms*
6 cups (1.5 litres) just-boiled water
   (from the kettle)
500g mixed mushrooms, sliced
   (I used Swiss brown, portabello, and
   white button)
1 tbsp extra virgin olive oil, plus
   2 tsp extra
3 thyme sprigs
100g unsalted butter
1 leek, white part finely chopped
2 garlic cloves, finely chopped
3 black garlic cloves*, finely chopped
1½ cups (330g) arborio rice
50g pecorino, finely grated, plus
   extra to serve
truffle oil (optional) and chervil,
   to serve

*Specialty ingredients
Porcini mushrooms are hard to get fresh but luckily the dried variety is more accessible. Found in most good delis. Black garlic can be found again at most good delis. It's roasted at a low temperature and tastes like a caramelised version of garlic. Almost like you've scraped the bottom of a roasting pan and got all the good bits of a roast.

Place stock cube, porcini and boiling water in a saucepan over low heat for 10 minutes to soak.

Preheat oven to 180°C fan forced. Grease and line a baking tray with baking paper.

Place mushrooms on prepared tray and drizzle with oil and scatter with thyme and salt and pepper. Bake for 15 minutes, or until golden.

Meanwhile, melt the butter in a large, wide, heavy-based frypan over medium heat. Add leek and cook for 5 minutes, or until softened. Add garlics, rice and extra oil and cook for 3 minutes to toast and coat each grain. Ladle in 2 cups of mushroom stock and stir to combine. Cook, gently stirring occasionally, until most of the liquid has been absorbed. Add another half a cup of stock and continue the process, adding the remaining stock half a cup at a time until rice is cooked through and has absorbed most of the liquid. Usually this takes around 20 minutes. Remove from heat and stir through pecorino and most of the mushrooms. Season with salt and pepper.

Divide among serving bowls and top with remaining mushrooms and drizzle with truffle oil, if using. Scatter with herbs and pecorino.

use it up
Leftover risotto makes for great arancini! Roll into balls, poke a cube of mozzarella cheese into the centre, then crumb like you would the chicken schnitty (page 212). Fry in 5cm of oil heated to 180°C for 3–4 minutes, or until golden.

meat lovers
A grilled chicken breast sliced and served on top of the risotto is a perfect finish for this scrummy plate of food.

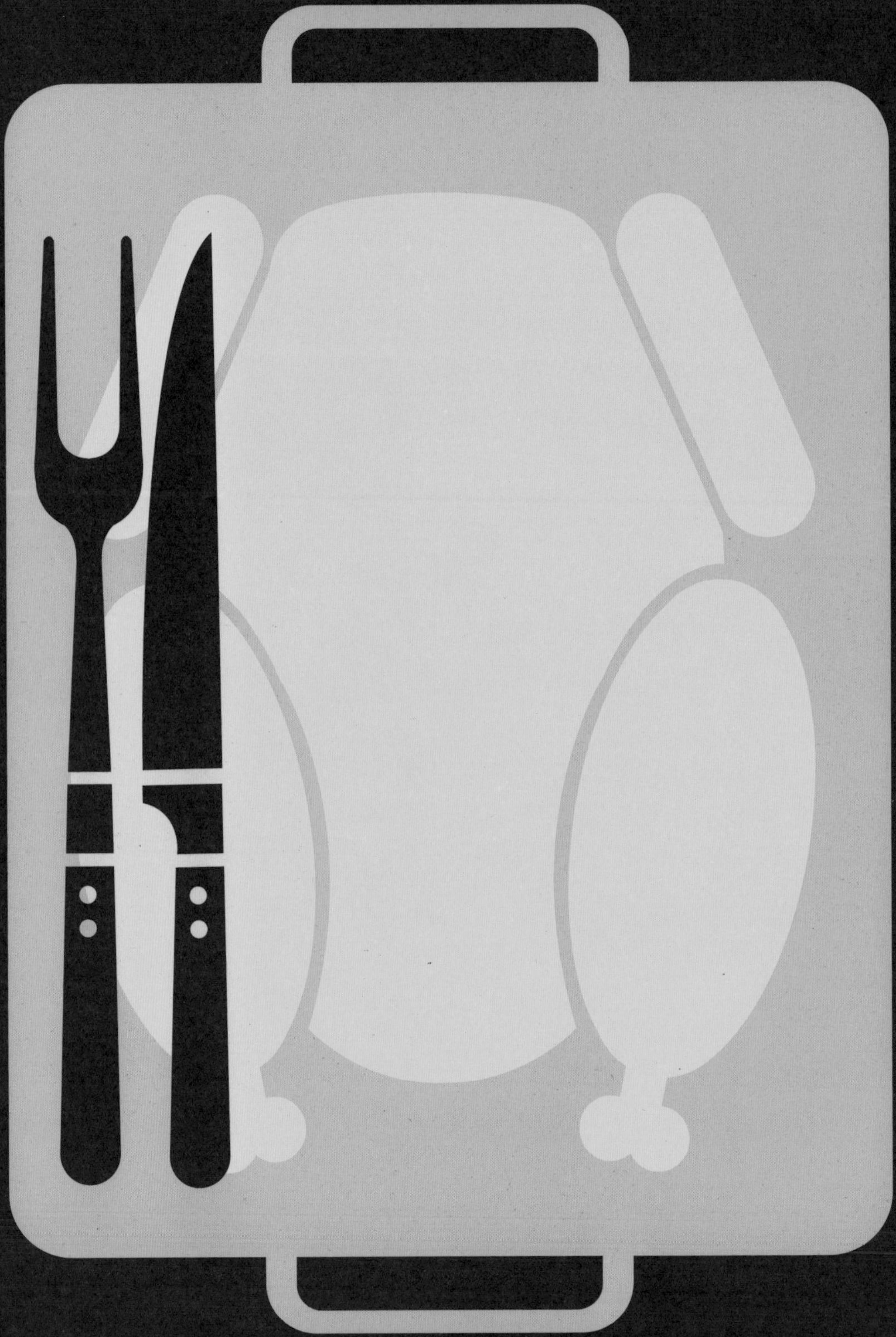

ROAST CHOOK

Winner winner, chicken dinner – these recipes are chook obsessed.
All parts tender and all skin crisp. Cluck cluck.

SLAP IT TOGETHER

chopped chook
salad
(pg 150)

GO TO

sweet chilli chicken
tray bake
(pg 152)

LONG GAME

leggy roast chook
and stuffing
(pg 154)

chopped chook salad

This salad is all about convenience. Born out of the classic rotisserie chook and the bag it comes in, it can be served hot or cold, shaken not stirred. Once shaken, this salad comes to life! Enjoy as a side or stuffed into rolls.

 effort 1/5   serves 4–6   prep 10 min

1 store-bought cooked chook or leftover roast chook, shredded
400g can black beans, rinsed and drained
100g sundried tomatoes in oil, sliced, plus 2 tbsp marinating oil
60g baby rocket leaves
1 cup (160g) frozen corn, blanched (or sub with canned)
200g Tasty cheese, cut into small cubes
1 punnet cherry tomatoes, quartered
1 avocado, diced
1 tbsp wholegrain mustard
juice of 1 lemon
1 small red onion, finely chopped
2 cups (140g) crispy fried noodles

Place shredded chicken in a lidded container (or use the bag it came cooked in). Add beans and sundried tomatoes and shake to mix. Add rocket, corn, cheese, cherry tomatoes and avocado and don't shake until you're ready to serve.

Combine mustard, lemon juice, onion and marinating oil in a jar.

When ready to serve, pour some of the dressing onto the salad and shake. Serve scattered with crispy noodles and remaining dressing alongside.

 m8s with — Fruit and nut brownie for picnic vibes (page 256).

 spice it up — I'm all about the sub-ins with a chicken salad. Swap out the Tasty cheese for feta or smoked Cheddar. Change the beans for chickpeas or lentils, or throw in some dukkah or za'atar for a different flavour profile.

sweet chilli chicken tray bake

Tray bakes just get me: less fuss, less washing up, but max flavour. Chop, toss and bake, that's all that's involved in this one. The sticky gnarly chicken that comes from roasting with the sweet chilli will have you licking your fingers and asking for more.

effort 2/5	gluten free	serves 4	prep 5 min	cook 1 hr

800g chicken thigh cutlets or legs, skin-on
⅓ cup (80ml) sweet chilli sauce
800g orange kūmara/sweet potato, cut into wedges
12 Brussels sprouts, halved
6 spring onions, thinly sliced, white part separated
100g snow peas, shredded
toasted sesame seeds, lime wedges and steamed rice, to serve

Toss chicken, sweet chilli sauce, kūmara/sweet potato, Brussels and white part of the spring onion in a bowl. (Marinate overnight if you have time.)

Preheat oven to 180°C fan forced. Grease and line a large baking tray with baking paper.

Transfer marinated chicken, skin side up, and veg onto the tray and arrange so that the veg is cut-side down (especially Brussels). Roast for 50 minutes–1 hour, or until chicken is cooked through.

Boil a kettle of water. Place snow peas in a heatproof bowl and pour over boiling water, let stand for 3 minutes, then drain.

Scatter snow peas, green spring onion and sesame seeds over chicken. Serve with lime wedges and rice alongside.

make it vegan Subbing in some firm tofu and raw cashews for the chicken makes for a tasty plant-based tray bake.

use it up I like to buy whole chickens and break them down. This recipe is a great one for the legs, wings and thighs. The frames I throw in a pot with veggie trimmings for stock and I use the breasts for laksa (page 76), Sounds like a lot of effort but once you've done it a few times it's pretty straightforward and saves a bit of coin at the checkout for that extra block of chocolate. Yes please.

leggy roast chook and stuffing

This is a roast chook to feed a crowd – everyone gets a leg – and the stuffing is baked-in and oozing with flavour. Sundays are sorted, and the leftovers that come from it, well where do I start . . . FYI, I start down below, or page 294, with 'love your leftovers'.

effort 3/5	serves 8	prep 30 min	cook 1 hr

150g butter, melted
¼ cup (80g) apricot jam
2 tbsp Worcestershire sauce
400g sourdough, torn into pieces
1 brown onion, thinly sliced
70g pecans, finely chopped
1 cup (250ml) chicken stock
1 egg, lightly beaten
6 garlic cloves, thinly sliced
2 sprigs rosemary, leaves picked
1kg chicken drumsticks
1 lemon, halved
1.2kg whole chicken
2 tbsp olive oil
¼ cup (35g) cranberries, chopped

Preheat oven to 200°C fan forced. Grease and line a heavy-based roasting pan with baking paper.

Combine, butter, jam and Worcestershire sauce. Transfer half a cup to a bowl along with bread, onion, pecans, stock, egg and half the garlic and rosemary. Mix with hands to combine well, squishing between fingers. Transfer to roasting pan.

Arrange drumsticks over stuffing. Place lemon and remaining garlic and rosemary inside whole chicken and use a skewer or kitchen string to hold legs together. Place in the centre of the pan. Drizzle with oil and season with salt and pepper.

Roast for 50 minutes or until chicken is golden and almost cooked through. Brush chicken and legs with remaining jam butter mixture and return to the oven for 10–15 minutes or until the juice runs clear when the thickest part of a thigh is pierced with a skewer and chicken is golden. Scatter over cranberries and serve immediately, for carving at the table.

use it up
Keep all of the bones, for stock. It doesn't have to be anything fancy, but to have some enriched liquid you can throw into rice or use to cook noodles or pasta – it's just a handy way to inject some flavour into your cooking at home!

prep ahead
Have this prepped and ready to go in the fridge up to 2 days in advance and trust me it will taste even better. The flavours will marinate, the chicken skin will dry out. All the good things will happen so when you switch on that oven and it hits the hot heat, it will know exactly what to do.

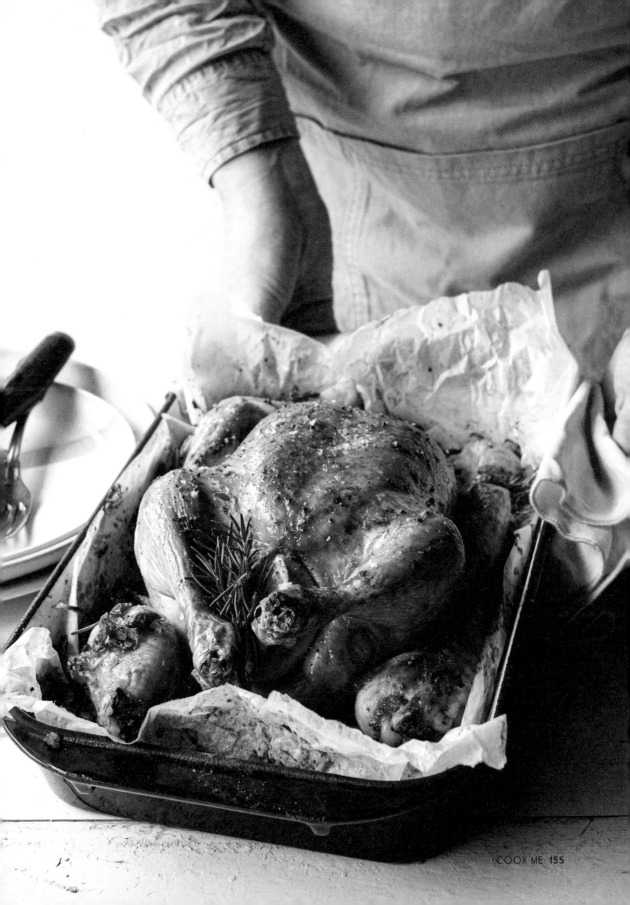

Hi!
On the off chance you've
landed on this centrefold
while perusing the
cookbooks, I just wanted
to say hello, you look
fabulous and you should
definitely buy me.
I'm all about maximum of
flavour and minimum of fuss.
Aren't we all? So, obviously
this is the book for you.
But please, keep flicking
and perusing – I'm sure the
photos will win you over. If you
have already bought the
book and are reading this,
thank you – people like
you are just the best.

FISH

Growing up camping by the seaside every summer of my life must have played some role in my taste for the sea. But there's no need to pull out the lobster; a can of tuna or a fish cake and I am good to go. Please note: throw in a gin and tonic for sundowners and I am SUPER good to go.

SLAP IT TOGETHER

tuna rice bowl
pg 160)

GO TO

sticky harissa
glazed salmon
(pg 162)

LONG GAME

Nana's fish cakes
(pg 164)

tuna rice bowl

This is basic, I am fully aware of that. But I am team basic when it comes to food, and this tuna rice bowl with microwaveable rice is the 5-minute secret lunch I wish I knew about at uni. (Instead, I was wasting my money on $10 lemongrass beef subs in ridiculously crunchy baguettes and crying poor when I'd go out on weekends – I actually regret nothing, but this would have been a good lunch, too.)

 effort 2/5 gluten free serves 2 prep 10 min cook 5 min

1 cup (160g) frozen shelled edamame
425g can tuna in olive oil, drained
1 small red onion, finely chopped
¼ cup (60g) Kewpie mayo, plus
   extra to serve
2 tbsp light soy sauce
1 tbsp shredded pickled (sushi)
   ginger, and 2 tbsp pickling liquid
1 tbs toasted sesame seeds, plus
   extra to serve
¼ tsp shichimi togarashi*, plus
   extra to serve
500g microwave rice
1 tbsp rice wine vinegar
4 radishes, thinly sliced
1 avocado, chopped
1 carrot, shredded
1 cucumber, thinly sliced
crushed wasabi peas*

*Specialty ingredients
*Wasabi peas, those coated crisp
green things you never knew you
needed as a bar snack, and shichimi
togarashi, a Japanese chilli spice mix,
are both found in Japanese and
Asian grocers.*

Boil the kettle. Place edamame in a saucepan. Pour over boiling water and place over high heat. Return to the boil, then drain.

Combine, tuna, onion, mayo, soy, ginger, pickling liquid, sesame seeds and togarashi in a bowl.

Heat rice as per packet instructions, add vinegar and shake to combine. Divide rice among bowls. Add radish, avocado, carrot, cucumber and edamame. Top with tuna mixture. Scatter with wasabi peas and serve with extra mayo and togarashi.

 spice it up
Mix some kimchi through the rice for a tasty fermented sitch. Balanced out with the creamy mayo and tuna, it's a tasty combo!

 jazz it up
Sub the can of tuna for some fresh sashimi-grade salmon, diced or sliced. Total winner.

sticky harissa glazed salmon

This is the recipe to use when entertaining. It's easy, packs flavour, feeds a crowd and is on that level where someone is sure to ask for the recipe (and in turn think you're amazing). Totally understand if you want to claim it, no need to mention me — because I imagine you've bought them my book anyways for secret Santa.

effort 1/5 | gluten free | serves 8–12 | prep 5 min | cook 12 min

⅓ cup (80ml) runny honey
⅓ cup (80ml) extra virgin olive oil, plus extra for drizzling
1 tbsp harissa spice mix or paste*
800g skin-on side of salmon (pin-boned preferred)
finely grated zest of 1 lemon, plus wedges to serve
mint, parsley and coriander, to serve

*Specialty ingredient
Harissa paste and spice mix is a perfect medley of roast peppers, tomato, garlic, coriander, cumin, lemon. It's a great ingredient to have in the pantry for a huge whack of flavour and can be found in good green grocers and delis.

Preheat oven to 200°C fan forced. Grease and line a baking tray with baking paper.

Combine honey, oil and harissa in a bowl. Place salmon on baking tray, skin-side in contact with tray, and pour over honey mixture. Roast, basting with sauce halfway, for 12 minutes, or until just cooked through. Remove and serve scattered with zest, herbs and lemon wedges alongside.

spice it up
You can sub the harissa with miso, gochujang, sriracha, ras-el-hanout or tomato paste. Salmon loves flavour and will take on whatever you throw at it.

jazz it up
Pomegranate seeds scattered over or some summer fruit like peaches grilled and added to the pan to glaze towards the end could truly set this off at a BBQ!

LONG GAME

Nana's fish cakes

My nana, a total foodie, made a version of these when growing up – she also made cream cheese and glacé ginger sandwiches and if that's not a genius combo I don't know what is. These fish cakes are total delicious comfort food for me. I like to make a big batch and have them in the freezer. They can also be baked and served with extra mashed potatoes and tomato sauce for a dollop of nostalgia.

 effort 3/5   makes 6   prep 15 min   cook 25 min

500g floury potatoes (usually the dirty ones), peeled and quartered
½ brown onion, finely chopped
1 garlic clove, bruised
2 bay leaves
1 tsp flaky salt
150g salmon or firm white fish fillet, chopped into 2cm chunks
200g hot smoked salmon pieces
finely grated zest of 1 lemon
1 egg
handful of chopped herbs – dill, or parsley works here
½ tsp cracked pepper
½ cup (75g) plain flour
oil to shallow fry
capers, mayo, salad and lemon wedges, to serve

Place potato, onion, garlic, bay leaves and salt in a saucepan and cover with cold water. Bring to the boil and cook for 15 minutes, or until cooked through. Add fresh fish and cook for a further 3 minutes. Strain, discard bay leaves and transfer to a bowl.

Mash, or whack around the bowl with a wooden spoon, to break up. Add hot smoked salmon, lemon zest, egg, herbs and pepper and mix to combine. Add flour and mix until mixture can be shaped to come together – add a bit more flour if you think it needs it.

Divide mixture into 6 and shape into large patties. Transfer to a plate and chill for at least 30 minutes to stiffen slightly.

Heat oil in a large frypan over medium-low heat and cook fish cakes, turning halfway, for 8 minutes, or until golden and cooked through. Serve with capers, mayo, salad and lemon wedges.

 spice it up Add 2 tbsp sambal oelek, 1 tsp green curry paste and finely chopped makrut lime leaf and these have a whole new flavour profile, perfect for wrapping in lettuce leaves and serving with herbs and bean sprouts for freshness.

 no fry Spray and bake in the oven at 200°C fan forced for 10 minutes, turning halfway, until cooked through and golden.

EGG

When in doubt, put an egg on it, or crack an egg into it, or enclose eggs in pastry and bake it. An egg, cooked in any form, is always a good idea.

SLAP IT TOGETHER
baked egg
chorizo beans
(pg 168)

GO TO
egg and shroom on
doorstop toast
(pg 170)

LONG GAME
zucchini slice . . .
but quiche
(pg 172)

baked egg chorizo beans

Born out of my obsession with canned baked beans with a fried egg, these beans hit all the brunch goals and come with soldiers for dipping. Popped in the middle of the table and ready in 20 minutes, you can win the morning with these beans.

effort 2/5 · veg · serves 4 · prep 5 min · cook 20 min

¼ cup (60ml) olive oil
1 brown onion, chopped
1 sprig rosemary, plus extra to serve
100g cured chorizo, thinly sliced
2 garlic cloves, sliced
2 x 400g cans cannellini beans, rinsed and drained
680g passata
2 tbsp smoky BBQ sauce
1 tbsp sherry vinegar
4 eggs
toast cut into soldiers, to serve

Heat oil in a large frypan over medium-high heat. Add onion, rosemary and chorizo and cook, stirring, for 5–6 minutes, or until softened and chorizo is beginning to crisp. Add garlic and cook for 1–2 minutes. Add beans and stir to coat, then add passata, BBQ sauce and vinegar and bring to the boil. Reduce to a simmer and cook for 5 minutes or until reduced slightly.

Use a wooden spoon to create indents in beans and crack eggs in. Cover and cook on low heat for 6–8 minutes, or until eggs are just cooked through, with a still-runny yolk. Remove lid and scatter with extra rosemary and a good cracking of pepper. Serve with toast for dipping in.

make it veg — Lose the chorizo and sub in some smoked paprika.

spice it up — Throw in some chipotle chilli puree to heat things up and serve with tortillas and smashed avo.

egg and shroom on doorstop toast

Don't you just want to poke the yolk?! It's the garlic in this that brings the shrooms to life. This also doubles as an awesome shroom sauce if you're looking for something to top your schnitty.

 effort 2/5 veg serves 2 prep 10 min cook 10 min

40g butter
2 tbsp olive oil
3 garlic cloves, thinly sliced
200g sliced mushrooms
2 tbsp Worcestershire sauce
⅓ cup (80ml) cream
few sprigs of thyme
2 doorstop-thick slices sourdough,
   toasted
2 eggs
finely grated Parmesan and
   some greenery, to serve (I went
   with rocket)

Heat butter and 1 tablespoon oil in a frypan over medium-high heat until melted. Add garlic and mushrooms to pan and cook for 5 minutes, or until softened and golden on the edges. Add Worcestershire, cream, thyme and a splash of water. Bring to the boil and cook for 1 minute.

When cooked, spoon over toast. Return pan to heat with remaining oil.

Crack in eggs and cook for 3–4 minutes, or until cooked to your liking. Transfer to toast and scatter with Parmesan and greenery to serve.

 use it up
Go for whatever mushrooms are seasoning the shelves. This can go in any direction: shitake, oyster, king brown or portobello. You can even throw in some zucchini or spinach leaves for bulk veg.

 meat lovers
I mean I never say no to some bacon.

zucchini slice . . . but quiche

Nothing worse than not having enough filling for a quiche. So, this is written to give a little extra. Thrown in a muffin tray you've got yourself a quiche with some complimentary frittatas – you're welcome. Also, how good is quiche. Wish it didn't get eaten so fast.

1 brown onion, finely chopped
150g streaky bacon, thinly sliced
2 garlic cloves, finely chopped
few sprigs thyme, chopped
8 eggs
1½ cups (125g) grated cheese
250g zucchini (approx. 3), coarsely
  grated, plus 1 extra, thinly sliced,
  to serve
⅓ cup (50g) self-raising flour
finely grated zest and juice of 1 lemon
60g rocket leaves
1 tbsp olive oil
caramelised onion relish, to serve

Short pastry
2 cups (300g) plain flour
150g salted butter, cut into cubes
½ tsp salt and white pepper
2 tsp English mustard
2 tbsp ice-cold water, plus more
  as required

Preheat oven to 200°C fan forced. Line a baking tray with baking paper.

For the pastry, place flour, butter, salt and pepper in the bowl of a food processor and whiz until the consistency of breadcrumbs. Add mustard and ice-cold water and pulse until the dough forms a ball. Shape into a disk. Dust a clean work surface with flour and use a rolling pin to roll out pastry to 4mm thickness. Use to line a 23cm quiche pan and push the pastry into the sides of the dish, leaving the overhang.

Chill for 30 minutes or until pastry is cold and firm. Once chilled, use a sharp knife to trim the sides. Use a fork to prick the base.

Place baking paper on top of pastry, fill with baking weights (or rice/dried beans) and place on prepared baking tray. Pop onion, bacon and garlic and thyme in the middle of a separate piece of baking paper and drizzle with oil. Scrunch up like a pudding and place on tray with pastry. Bake both for 25 minutes, or until the sides of the pastry are golden. Remove bacon mixture, paper and pastry weights. Return the pastry to the oven for 10 minutes, or until golden all over.

Meanwhile, combine bacon mixture, eggs, cheese, zucchini and flour in a bowl. Pour into baked pastry so it's so full it could burst, then spoon any remaining mixture into a lined muffin tray for muffin frittatas. Reduce oven to 170°C and bake the quiche and muffins for 30–35 minutes, or until egg mix has set and cheese is golden.

Toss extra zucchini slices, rocket, lemon zest and juice and oil in a bowl.

Serve quiche with salad and relish on the side.

 Lose the bacon and use a smoked Cheddar instead to bring that smokiness.

 Any leftover pastry can be rolled out scattered with Parmesan and baked for cheesy crackers.

LEAFY SALAD

You can make friends with salad — mainly because a salad prepared by someone else always tastes better, so yeah, your friends will love it. Also, these salads are yumbles.

SLAP IT TOGETHER

iceberg chunk salad with buttermilk dressing
(pg 176)

GO TO

kaley no-mayo warm slaw
(pg 178)

LONG GAME

ultimate caesar salad with jammy eggs
(pg 180)

iceberg chunk salad
with buttermilk dressing

The simplest salad there ever was but packed with flavour. The key is letting the dressing soak in just enough so the iceberg just softens into the flavour and becomes a carrier for deliciousness – it sounds technical but it's literally just dressing it and waiting 5 minutes before serving.

effort 1/5 · veg · serves 4–6 as a side · prep 10 min

1 iceberg lettuce, cut into wedges
2 avocados, sliced
chervil and olive oil, to serve

Buttermilk dressing
½ cup (125ml) buttermilk
2 tbsp mayo
2 tsp onion powder
1 garlic clove, finely grated
finely grated zest and juice of 1 lemon
1 bunch chives, thinly sliced
1 tsp freshly cracked pepper

For the dressing, place all ingredients in a jar and shake to combine.

Arrange wedges of lettuce on a serving dish. Spoon over dressing and wait 5 minutes to soak in slightly. Scatter with avocado and chervil and drizzle with olive oil to serve.

spice it up Some miso In the dressing and shichimi togarashi to scatter takes this into a really fun place.

prep ahead This dressing can be made in advance and kept in the fridge for up to 1–2 weeks. Just give him a good shake before using.

kaley no-mayo warm slaw

This is how we make kale the hero: drench it in flavour and marry it with friends, like carrot, cabbage, and mango and pepper it with raisins and pumpkin seeds.

 effort 3/5 vegan serves 4–6 as a side prep 15 min cook 7 min

¼ cup (60ml) extra virgin olive oil
2 tsp nigella seeds
1 tsp each cumin and caraway seeds
2 garlic cloves, finely grated
1 tsp flaky salt
½ bunch kale, leaves shredded, stems finely sliced (kept separate)
¼ cup (60ml) apple cider vinegar
2 tbsp water
1 tbsp wholegrain mustard
200g (approx. ¼) savoy cabbage, shredded
200g (approx. ¼) red cabbage, shredded
1 carrot, shredded
1 apple or green mango, sliced
juice of 1 lemon
2 tbsp each chopped raisins and toasted pumpkin seeds
small handful dill sprigs or fennel fronds, to serve

Heat oil in a wok or large frypan over high heat. Add nigella, cumin, caraway, garlic and salt and cook for 1–2 minutes, or until aromatic. Add kale stems and cook, stirring, for 2–3 minutes, or until softened slightly. Add kale leaves, vinegar and water and cook, stirring, for 2 minutes to soften slightly. Remove from heat and stir through remaining ingredients.

Season to taste and stack onto a serving plate and scatter with dill or fennel. Spoon over any remaining dressing from the pan to serve, warm or cold.

 jazz it up — Flake through some hot smoked salmon and a few boiled eggs for a super-wholesome feed.

 use it up — Feel free to use up all the bits from the fridge, fruit bowl or random harvests from the garden. Kale loves a party.

ultimate caesar salad
with jammy eggs

What is it about a Caesar salad that hits all the taste buds? The crunchy lettuce, tangy dressing, jammy egg – or is it just the fact that there's bacon to round everything out . . .? Whatever it may be, Caesar is a total pleaser so you can't go wrong with this one.

 effort 3/5 serves 4 prep 20 min cook 20 min

8 eggs
iced water
8 slices bacon
300g sourdough bread, thinly
  sliced and torn
1 tbsp olive oil
2 baby cos lettuce, torn into
  bite-size pieces

Ultimate Caesar dressing
2 egg yolks
1 tbsp Dijon mustard
20g Parmesan, finely grated, plus
  extra to serve
1–2 garlic cloves, finely grated
6 anchovies, in oil
2 tsp Worcestershire sauce
½ tsp cracked pepper
finely grated zest and juice of 1 lemon
2 tbsp apple cider vinegar
¼ cup (60ml) extra virgin olive oil
1 cup (250ml) vegetable oil
2 tbsp water

To make the jammy eggs, bring a saucepan of water to the boil. Add eggs and cook for 6 minutes and 30 seconds. Strain and plunge into bowl of iced water. Peel.

Meanwhile, preheat oven to 200°C fan forced, and grease and line a baking tray with baking paper. Add the bacon, bread and drizzle with oil. Bake for 15 minutes or until bread is crisp and bacon is charred slightly.

For the dressing, place egg yolks, Dijon, Parmesan, garlic, anchovies, Worcestershire sauce, pepper, lemon zest and juice and vinegar in a food processor and whiz to combine until pale. With the motor running slowly add the oils until thick and emulsified. Stir through water, one tablespoon at a time, to loosen. Season to taste.

Arrange lettuce, bacon, sourdough and halved eggs across plates or on one large serving plate. Pour over some of the dressing and serve immediately showered in extra Parmesan and remaining dressing alongside.

 meat lovers
Throw in some chicken schnitty (page 212) or the leftovers from the leggy roast chook (page 154).

 prep ahead
The dressing can be made and kept in a jar or airtight container for 1–2 weeks! Something about having the dressing ready makes this salad 10 times more achievable on a weeknight.

LESS LETTUCE SALAD

These are salads that treat lettuce as a mere afterthought in their composition. It's like the third cousin who invited themselves to your Christmas lunch but brings a really good dessert. You're happy to have them there, but I guess they weren't your first pick. I have a third cousin though who's a lovely human so that doesn't apply to me.

SLAP IT TOGETHER

watermelon salad
(pg 184)

GO TO

maple roasted pumpkin
and couscous salad
with raisin dressing
(pg 186)

LONG GAME

broccoli salad with
falafel crumb
(pg 188)

watermelon salad

This salad is so fresh, so easy and so full of flavour it's hard to not pull it out for any and all gatherings. If watermelon is in season, this is the only salad you should be making.

 effort 1/5   veg   gluten free   serves 4–6 as a side   prep 15 min

1kg watermelon, cut into cubes
2 Lebanese cucumbers, sliced
100g Kalamata olives, thinly sliced
200g Greek-style feta, thinly sliced
⅓ cup (80ml) extra virgin olive oil
zest and juice of 2 lemons
2 tsp dried Greek oregano
½ bunch mint, leaves picked
½ bunch basil, leaves picked (I used baby Greek basil)

Place watermelon, cucumber, olives and feta on a serving platter. Combine oil, lemon juice and zest and dried oregano and season to taste. Pour over salad and top with herbs to serve.

 m8s with — Grilled squid with taramasalata (page 204)

 more veg please — Throw in some cherry tomatoes and diced capsicum for an almost-Greek salad.

 use it up — If there are any leftovers, whiz up to make a really fun cold soup/dressing.

maple roasted pumpkin and couscous salad
with raisin dressing

I'm so hooked on roasting pumpkin like this. Standing it up so its end bits get all burnt and gnarly, then coating in a maple spiced glaze. It's the only way to roast pumpkin if you ask me, and this raisin dressing it's partnered with is an absolute winner — it's a good one to have up your sleeve for any kind of salad.

effort 3/5 · **veg** · **serves 4–6** as a side · **prep** 10 min · **cook** 45 min

1 tbsp smoked paprika
2 tbsp maple syrup
⅓ cup (80ml) olive oil
½ pumpkin, cut into 3cm-thick wedges
1 cup (200g) couscous
finely grated zest of 1 lemon (use the juice in the dressing)
1½ cups (375ml) boiling water
100g spinach leaves
1 punnet cherry tomatoes, halved
dill sprigs, to serve

Raisin dressing
⅓ cup (55g) golden raisins
⅓ cup (80ml) white wine vinegar
⅓ cup (80ml) extra virgin olive oil
2 garlic cloves
1 tbsp capers
2 anchovies in oil
2 tsp Dijon mustard
1 long green chilli, halved (seeds removed if you don't want too much heat)
juice of 1 lemon
½ bunch parsley, plus extra to serve

Preheat oven to 200°C fan forced. Grease and line a baking tray with baking paper.

Combine paprika, maple, 2 tablespoons of oil and a good pinch of salt and pepper in a large bowl. Add pumpkin slices and toss to coat. Transfer to tray, sitting upright (reserving the excess paprika oil), and bake for 40 minutes, or until cooked through and gnarly. Meanwhile, put the remnants of the paprika oil and couscous into a bowl along with lemon zest and remaining oil. Stir to coat the grains, then add boiling water. Cover and stand until required.

For the dressing, place everything in a blender and whiz until smooth and green.

Transfer pumpkin to a serving platter. Fluff couscous and stir through a few tablespoons of dressing. Spoon over pumpkin, scatter with spinach, tomatoes and dill and serve with remaining dressing alongside.

spice it up Turn up the heat on the pumpkin and throw in some chilli flakes or Kashmiri chilli powder.

use it up For the dressing, sub the parsley for any herbs you have or want to use up. I'm talking about all the end bits in your crisper we all have. Everything gets blended together anyways so it's perfect for giving them a new lease on life.

broccoli salad
with falafel crumb

I absolutely hated broccoli when I was a kid. But now, spoiler alert, it's probably one of my favourite foods. My standards for broc have changed though: it's always dressed to the nines with lemon juice and olive oil and seasoned well. Otherwise, we cannot be seen together. Shout out to the falafel crumb in this salad! Make a double batch and scatter it over any and all things #gamechangercrumb.

effort 3/5 · veg · gluten free · serves 4–6 as a side · prep 20 min · cook 20 min

2 heads broccoli, stems sliced, head
   cut into bite-size pieces
¼ cup (60ml) extra virgin olive oil,
   plus extra to serve
finely grated zest and juice of 1 lemon
¼ red onion, thinly sliced
1 cup (250g) labneh*

Falafel halloumi crumb
400g can chickpeas, rinsed and
   drained
250g halloumi, chopped
½ brown onion, chopped
1 garlic clove, chopped
½ bunch each of parsley and
   coriander, chopped
1 tsp each ground cumin and
   coriander
olive oil spray

***Specialty ingredients**
*Labneh is a thick strained yoghurt
found in Middle Eastern grocers.
You can make your own by spooning
yoghurt into a sieve lined with muslin
or a brand new CHUX wipe and hang
it over a bowl in the fridge overnight
to strain the whey, leaving a thick,
delicious labneh.*

Preheat oven to 220°C fan forced. Grease and line a baking tray with baking paper.

For the falafel crumb, place everything in a food processor and whiz until finely chopped. Transfer to a baking tray and spray with oil. Bake, stirring halfway, for 15 minutes, or until golden and crisp.

Bring a saucepan of water to the boil. Add broccoli and cook for 4–5 minutes, or until just tender. Drain and rinse under cold water to refresh. Transfer to a bowl along with oil, lemon juice and zest, onion and seasoning. Toss to coat.

To assemble, spoon labneh onto a serving dish. Add broccoli mixture and then spoon over falafel crumb.

make it vegan Ditch the labneh and sub the halloumi for 1 tbsp tahini. Serve with the hummus out of the loaded meatball hummus (page 32).

spice it up Broc does well with spice, so a pinch of chilli flakes in here can really send it!

VEG FOR-WARD

These recipes are all about letting the veggies shine. There could easily be more than three recipes in here but I chose three of the best to show off just how damn magical vegetables are. Please be upstanding for these three legends: corn, eggplant and cauliflower. May they always be tender and coated in tasty things.

SLAP IT TOGETHER
loaded corn cobs
(pg 192)

GO TO
gochujang-glazed eggplant with chippies
(pg 194)

LONG GAME
butter cauliflower
(pg 196)

loaded corn cobs

I should have called these swarm cobs. Cos once they're finished with grated Parmesan, watch as people swarm! Such a simple combo of flavours and a classic on any Mexican menu. These cobs of glory are a welcome treat to have at home. I just love how they get to have a little soak in the 'bath' (read sink) first – trust me, it helps with steaming.

6 whole corns, husks intact
⅔ cup (160ml) mayo
1 tbsp sriracha
½ tsp smoked paprika, plus extra
   to serve
finely grated zest and juice of 1 lime
50g finely grated Parmesan or
   pecorino
½ bunch coriander, leaves picked
finely sliced chives, to serve

Preheat oven to 180°C fan forced.

Submerge corn in water in a large pot or in a clean sink for 10 minutes to soak.

Transfer corn to a tray and bake, husk and all, for 45 minutes or until corn is tender and husks are darkened slightly.

Combine mayo, sriracha, paprika and lime zest and juice.

Remove corn and carefully pull down the husks. Transfer to a tray and add mayo, then shake to coat. Grate over Parmesan and scatter with paprika and herbs. Serve hot!

 The beer-batter fish burgers with tartare iceberg slaw (page 56).

 Finely dice some chorizo and cook it off in a pan, then spoon over the corn.

gochujang-glazed eggplant
with chippies

Salt and vin chips are the ultimate crunch-addition to this eggplant. Once you pop you will not stop. I could definitely eat two of these myself easily – but one per person is probably a normal-person portion, or a good side/share plate for two to four people.

effort 2/5 · veg · gluten free · serves 2 · prep 5 min · cook 30 min

2 eggplants, halved lengthways
½ tsp flaky salt
2 tbsp extra virgin olive oil, plus extra for drizzling
2 tbsp maple syrup
1 tbsp gochujang paste*
1 tbsp rice wine vinegar
1 tsp sesame oil
1 handful of salt and vinegar chips
chopped chives, thinly sliced red chilli, steamed rice and green thangs, like mesclun lettuce and stray herbs you want to get rid of, to serve

Specialty ingredient
Gochujang is a fermented Korean chilli paste that is balanced with sweetness. Found in any good Asian grocer.

Preheat oven to 200°C fan forced. Grease and line a baking tray with baking paper.

Score the inside flesh of each eggplant half with a knife 1cm deep in a criss-cross pattern. Sprinkle with salt and drizzle with oil. Massage into flesh, then place cut side down on prepared baking tray.

Bake for 20 minutes or until flesh is softened and the cut side is slightly golden.

Meanwhile, combine maple, gochujang, vinegar and sesame oil.

Flip cooked eggplant and spoon over glaze mixture to coat. Turn oven to grill on high and cook sauce side up for 10 minutes, or until golden and gnarly.

Crunch up chips and scatter over eggplant. Top with chives, chilli and green thangs. Serve hawt with steamed rice.

 spice it up — Sub the gochujang for miso, sriracha or even hoisin for a change in spicery.

 jazz it up — Slice and serve in a bowl with steamed short grain rice, edamame, corn, shaved radish and thinly sliced spring onion for a glazed-eggplant donburi bowl.

butter cauliflower

One of my all-time favourite curries, this is packed with flavour and will have you dipping, dipping and re-dipping (double dipper!) your naan. A celebration of spice, this curry is on heavy rotation for us!

 effort 3/5 veg serves 4–6 prep 15 min cook 30 min

2 tbsp oil
1 cauliflower, cut into eighths
⅓ cup (80g) ghee or butter
1 brown onion, finely chopped
4cm piece ginger, finely chopped
3 cloves garlic, chopped
400g can chickpeas, rinsed and
    drained
680g passata
1 cup (250ml) cream
juice of 1 lemon
naan bread and steamed rice, to serve

Butter up spice mix
3 tsps each ground cumin, ground
    coriander, Kashmiri chilli powder*
¼ tsp each ground nutmeg, cinnamon,
    black mustard seeds, ground cloves,
    ground cardamom
12 curry leaves

Specialty ingredient
*Kashmiri chilli powder is a variety of
chilli that is red in colour but more
mild in heat. It can be found in Indian
grocers.*

Preheat oven to 210°C fan forced. Line a baking tray with baking paper and drizzle with oil.

Put cauliflower pieces onto prepared tray cut side down. Season with salt and pepper. Bake for 20–25 minutes, or until golden and slightly charred.

Meanwhile, combine all ingredients for the spice mix in a small bowl.

Heat ghee or butter in a wide saucepan or deep-sided frypan over medium heat. Add onion and cook for 3 minutes, or until softened. Add ginger and garlic and spice mix and cook for a further 1–2 minutes, or until aromatic and seeds begin to pop. Add chickpeas, passata and cream and cook for 15 minutes, or until reduced slightly. Stir through lemon juice to taste. Add roasted cauliflower.

Serve with naan and steamed rice alongside.

 make it vegan — Sub the cream for cashew cream and boom! She's vegan.

 meat lovers — I throw no judgement if you feel like throwing some chicken in with the cauliflower and adding it to the sauce. I totally get that sometimes we want a little chicken in our butter . . . chicken.

CRILL ME

There's nothing like the aroma of a preheating BBQ grill. Or if you're lucky, a wood burner or hibachi grill. Grilling over high heat delivers crust, char and tenderness and delivers us that Maillard reaction and BBQ taste we all strive for. Feel free to use that term at your next BBQ; you'll have people nodding along like they know what's up.

SLAP IT TOGETHER

t-bone steak with *the* horseradish butter
(pg 202)

CO TO

grilled squid
with taramasalata
(pg 204)

LONG CAME

XO lamb skewers
with peanut butter
baba ganoush
(pg 206)

FLAVOU

aka a marinade, but I'm known for bathing my chicken overnight – or if I don't have time, showering it for 30mins–1 hour.

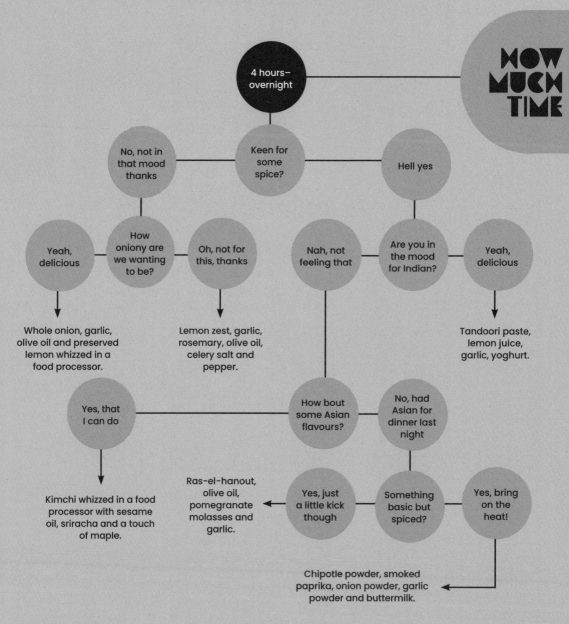

HOW MUCH TIME

4 hours– overnight

Keen for some spice?

No, not in that mood thanks

Hell yes

Yeah, delicious

How oniony are we wanting to be?

Oh, not for this, thanks

Nah, not feeling that

Are you in the mood for Indian?

Yeah, delicious

Whole onion, garlic, olive oil and preserved lemon whizzed in a food processor.

Lemon zest, garlic, rosemary, olive oil, celery salt and pepper.

Tandoori paste, lemon juice, garlic, yoghurt.

Yes, that I can do

How bout some Asian flavours?

No, had Asian for dinner last night

Kimchi whizzed in a food processor with sesame oil, sriracha and a touch of maple.

Ras-el-hanout, olive oil, pomegranate molasses and garlic.

Yes, just a little kick though

Something basic but spiced?

Yes, bring on the heat!

Chipotle powder, smoked paprika, onion powder, garlic powder and buttermilk.

R BATN

Here are some ideas for adding some more flavour to any piece of plain Jane (sorry Jane) meat, tofu, seafood and/or vegetable . . .

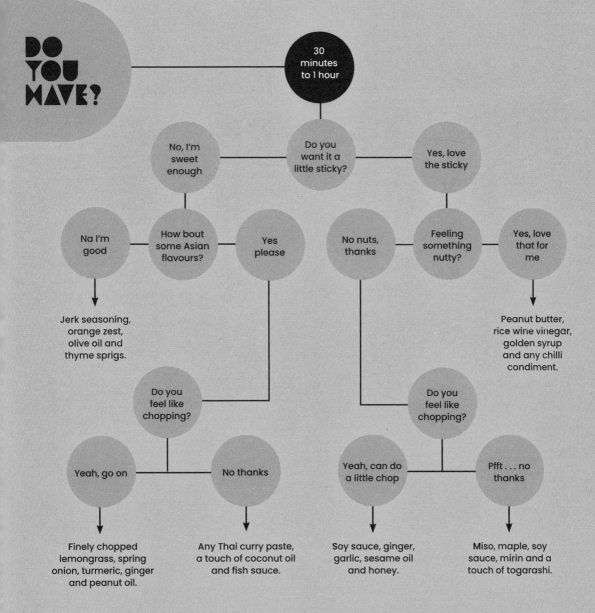

DO YOU HAVE?

30 minutes to 1 hour

Do you want it a little sticky?

No, I'm sweet enough

Yes, love the sticky

How bout some Asian flavours?

Na I'm good

Yes please

Feeling something nutty?

No nuts, thanks

Yes, love that for me

Na I'm good → Jerk seasoning, orange zest, olive oil and thyme sprigs.

Yes, love that for me → Peanut butter, rice wine vinegar, golden syrup and any chilli condiment.

Do you feel like chopping?

Yeah, go on

No thanks

Do you feel like chopping?

Yeah, can do a little chop

Pfft . . . no thanks

Yeah, go on → Finely chopped lemongrass, spring onion, turmeric, ginger and peanut oil.

No thanks → Any Thai curry paste, a touch of coconut oil and fish sauce.

Yeah, can do a little chop → Soy sauce, ginger, garlic, sesame oil and honey.

Pfft . . . no thanks → Miso, maple, soy sauce, mirin and a touch of togarashi.

t-bone steak
with *the* horseradish butter

Is butter, is better – I've always been pro-butter (mainly because it usually comes with bread) and this horseradish butter for steak is ridiculously tasty! The horseradish gives it a real kick as it pools with the butter smothered over the steak. Well, you'll just have to taste it and let me know what you think. Also, T-bone steak always: the flavour you get from the bone is undeniable. Think of it almost like a lamb cutlet, but three times the size. The royal of beef cuts if you ask me.

effort 2/5 | gluten free | serve 4 | prep 2 hr | cook 25 min

500g thick-cut T-bone steaks
2 tsp each flaky salt and cracked pepper
200g butter, chopped and softened
¼ cup (70g) horseradish cream
1 tbsp wholegrain mustard
1 tsp each onion and porcini powder
2 tbsp oil
chervil, to serve

Season steak with salt and cracked pepper. Stand at room temperature for at least 15 minutes (even better, 1 hour).

For the butter, whiz butter, horseradish, mustard, onion and porcini powder in a small food processor until combined. Keep at room temperature until ready to serve.

To cook the steak, heat a BBQ or grill pan over high heat. Drizzle steaks with oil and cook, without touching, for 4 minutes or until blood begins to show on the surface of the meat. Turn and cook for a further 4 minutes or until when pressed, the meat has the resistance of a firm mattress (lol).

Transfer to a plate and add a spoonful of butter and leave to rest for 10 minutes. Slice and serve scattered with chervil with extra butter alongside.

m&s with

Iceberg chunk salad with buttermilk dressing (page 176) and twice-cooked garlic lemon potatoes (page 86).

use it up

Compound butters are good at taking on whatever you want to throw at them, so this is a good one for using up what you have in the condiments section. Kimchi butter, caramelised onion relish butter, mustard butter – it's amazing what you can do with a few jars and a stick of butter.

grilled squid
with taramasalata

The richness of the taramasalata against the fresh lemon charred squid is a perfect balance of sea and land. A surf and turf, you could say – the turf being the lemon and parsley, which literally grow in the ground so probably more turfy than a steak if you ask me. Sub in a store-bought taramasalata if you're low on time! It's found in the dip section at the supermarket.

effort 3/5 · serves 4–6 as a starter · prep 30 min · cook 5 min

1kg whole squid, cleaned and
  skin removed
1 tsp white sugar
finely grated zest and juice of
  2 lemons
1 bunch parsley, leaves picked
  and finely chopped
⅓ cup (80ml) extra virgin olive oil,
  plus 2 tbsp extra
5 garlic cloves, thinly sliced
Grilled pita, to serve

Taramasalata
2 slices soft white bread, chopped
2 cups (500ml) water
½ small brown onion, roughly
  chopped
50g tarama* (cod roe paste)
finely grated zest and juice of
  1 lemon
pinch of sweet paprika
1 cup (250ml) vegetable oil

Specialty ingredient
Tarama is the salted and cured
roe of cod or carp, found in a can
in Greek delis. Trust me when I
say it's the butter of the sea.

For the taramasalata, soak the bread in water for 2 minutes, or until softened. Strain through a sieve and squeeze out the excess water. Transfer to a blender along with onion, tarama, lemon zest and juice and paprika and whiz until smooth. With the motor running, pour in the oil in a thin, steady stream until the mixture combines and becomes smooth. If the mixture is too thick, loosen it with warm water, 1 tablespoon at a time, until it reaches a thick, mayo-like consistency. Season to taste. Chill until required.

Remove the tentacles of the squid by cutting just below the head. Clean squid and discard head, then cut a slit along the side of the tube to reveal the inside. Score the inside with a sharp knife then again in the opposite direction. Cut into 6cm pieces.

Toss in a bowl with sugar and half the lemon juice. Stand for 10 minutes to tenderise slightly.

Combine parsley, lemon zest, oil and remaining lemon juice in a bowl.

Preheat BBQ or grill pan over high heat. It's important to get it almost smoking here. Drain and transfer squid to a tray and pat well with paper towel to dry out the surface. Drizzle with extra oil, scatter with garlic and cook on grill, turning frequently, for 1–2 minutes, or until charred, curled and opaque.

Transfer squid to bowl with parsley mixture and stir to coat.

Serve with taramasalata and grilled pita bread.

 spice it up Seafood loves chilli, so if everyone at the table approves feel free to throw in a little soy sauce and freshly sliced chilli.

 meat lovers Chorizo gives a great meaty vibe to this dish! Thinly sliced, it can get cooked at the same time as the squid.

XO lamb skewers
with peanut butter baba ganoush

I love me a skewer. Feel free to interchange the lamb here with chicken thigh fillets, beef rump, prawns or even tofu. But as biased as it may sound, lamb will always be my first choice. Also, and this is very important: this baba ganoush is outrageously good and I might have to sell it one day. But until then I give it to you to try and tell me how utterly delicious it is.

 effort 4/5 gluten free serves 4–6 prep 30 min cook 45 min

800g boneless lamb leg, cut into
 3cm pieces
1 tbsp XO sauce*, plus extra to serve
2 tbsp soy sauce
1 tsp ground turmeric
1½ tsp white sugar
1 tsp cumin seeds
1 red onion, thinly sliced
½ tsp flaky salt
2 tbsp olive oil, plus extra to serve
crushed peanuts and mint leaves
 to serve

Peanut butter baba ganoush
500g (approx. 2) eggplants
¼ cup (70g) peanut butter
2 garlic cloves
juice of 1 lemon, plus extra
 wedges to serve
1 tbsp olive oil
1 tsp sumac*, plus extra to serve

Specialty ingredients
*XO sauce is an umami condiment
made with dried seafood. It is found
at all good Asian grocers, usually
behind the counter as it's such a
prized ingredient. Sumac, made from
dried berries, is a tiny spice with huge
flavour and big citrus notes.*

Combine lamb, XO, soy, turmeric, sugar and cumin seeds in a bowl. Thread onto skewers and stand for at least 10 minutes – this allows the meat a chance to come to room temperature (30 minutes would be ideal if you have the time – go on.)

Meanwhile, to make the baba ganoush, pierce eggplant with a fork and roast on a BBQ or in a 220ºC fan forced oven for 40 minutes, turning halfway, or until eggplant is cooked through and blackened. Transfer to a bowl and cover and stand to steam for 10 minutes, or until cool enough to handle.

Reserve cooking liquid and peel away skin. Transfer flesh to a blender along with peanut butter, garlic, lemon juice and oil and up to 1 tablespoon of reserved eggplant liquid. Whiz until smooth. Spoon onto a serving dish and scatter with sumac. Chill until required.

Toss onion with salt and stand to soften slightly.

Heat a grill pan over high heat, drizzle skewers with oil and cook, in batches if necessary and turning frequently, for 6–8 minutes or until golden and caramelised on all the edges. Add to plate of baba ganoush and drizzle with oil.

Scatter with sumac, peanuts and mint sprigs, and serve with salted onion and lemon wedges.

 m8s with · Broccoli salad with falafel crumb (page 188).

 prep ahead · Both the baba ganoush and the skewers can be prepped ahead so all that's left to do is stand over the BBQ, with cold drink in hand.

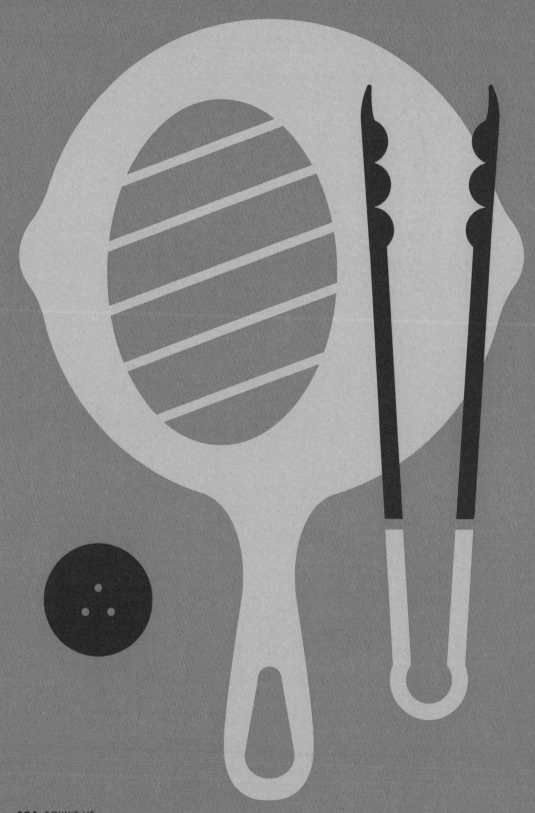

SCHNIT ME

Anything crumbed in bread (aka schnitzel) is an absolute winner in my book. The trick is getting flavour in there to make the effort of crumbing worth it! So go on, get schnitting. (It's safe to say I really held back with the schnit puns here, but schnit me they would have been good.)

SLAP IT TOGETHER

tandoori lamb
lollypops
(pg 210)

GO TO

chicken schnitty with
parsley lemon sauce
(pg 212)

LONG GAME

eggplant parmi
bake
(pg 214)

tandoori lamb lollypops

Tandoori lamb cutlets need no introduction, but these schnitz-style ones do. Ditching the egg and dredging in a yoghurt tandoori mixture keeps these lollypops on the lighter side and also makes the crumb process that little bit easier.

effort 2/5   **serves 6** as a starter   **prep** 5 min   **cook** 15 min

¼ cup (70g) tandoori paste*
1 cup (280g) thick Greek-style yoghurt
12 lamb cutlets
1½ cups (75g) panko breadcrumbs
olive oil spray
1 tsp Kashmiri chilli powder*
2 tsp flaky salt
1 tbsp coriander chutney*, thawed
date and tamarind chutney* and
  coriander leaves, to serve

*Specialty ingredients
Coriander chutney and date and tamarind chutney can be found in Indian grocers. The coriander chutney is more of a fresh style chutney and is sometimes made with mint also so is usually kept in the freezer whereas the tamarind chutney is in a jar and almost jam like. Grab the tandoori paste and Kashmiri chilli powder (a mild and vibrant red spice) while you're here also!

Preheat oven to 240°C fan forced. Grease and line a baking tray with baking paper and place a rack over the top.

Combine tandoori and half the yoghurt in a bowl. Put breadcrumbs in a separate bowl. Dip lamb into tandoori mix and spread to coat all over meat, avoiding the bone. Dip in breadcrumbs to coat meat completely, again avoiding bone, then transfer to rack and spray well with oil.

Bake, turning and spraying halfway, for 12 minutes, or until golden and lamb is cooked medium-rare. Combine Kashmiri chilli powder and salt in a bowl and use to season lamb.

Combine coriander chutney and remaining yoghurt in a bowl and serve alongside lamb cutlets with date and tamarind chutney, coriander leaves and extra chilli salt.

m8s with
The butter cauliflower (page 196), for obvious reasons.

more veg please
Some sliced fresh cucumber, tomatoes and mint sprigs tossed together for a quick fragrant salad would work well with these pops.

chicken schnitty
with parsley lemon sauce

Chicken schnitty: as an Aussie, it doesn't get any more pub meal than that. But I understand you may disagree, especially if you're a Kiwi, so here I've gone for a fresher route, with a tangy lemon parsley sauce that cuts through the crumb and takes this chicken to Delicious Town – yes, that's totally a place. This was on re-runs at our house growing up, hope it gets binged at yours too!

effort 3/5　serves 4　prep 20 min　cook 15 min

2 chicken breasts, halved horizontally
1 tsp Dijon mustard
1 cup (150g) plain flour
3 eggs
2 tbsp mayo
2 cups (100g) panko breadcrumbs
vegetable oil for shallow frying
2 cups (240g) frozen peas
100g marinated feta*, plus 1 tbsp
　marinating oil
1 bunch parsley, finely chopped
finely grated zest and juice of 2 lemons
pea tendrils, to serve

*Specialty ingredient
Marinated feta takes standard feta
up a notch. By buying it already
marinating in herbs and spices we
get another level of flavour which
brings the feta to life. Make sure to
keep the oil and use it in place of oil
in any savoury recipe!

Place chicken between two sheets of baking paper and use a rolling pin or mallet to whack out to 3mm thickness. Brush with Dijon. Put flour in a bowl, and whisk eggs and mayo together in another bowl. Scatter breadcrumbs over a large tray. Toss chicken in flour and and then dredge through egg and mayo mixture. Coat eggy chicken in breadcrumbs completely. Repeat with remaining pieces of chicken.

Heat 2cm of oil in a large frypan over medium heat. Working in batches, add crumbed chicken and cook, turning halfway, for 6–8 minutes, or until golden and cooked through.

Blanch peas and roughly squish in a bowl to break apart slightly. Add feta and marinating oil.

Combine parsley, lemon zest and juice and season to taste. Divide pea mix among plates and top with chicken. Spoon over lemon parsley and scatter with pea tendrils to serve.

spice it up

Add some togarashi to the crumb and serve with Japanese curry sauce for something a little spicy! You can find this curry sauce in little stock-style cubes in Asian grocers, and some supermarkets.

prep ahead

Totally make extra of these and freeze them! Spray them with oil and cook from frozen in a 180°C fan forced oven for 20–25 minutes, which is a great no-fry option regardless.

eggplant parmi bake

Eggplant is the ultimate veg at acting almost like meat. It has the juiciness, the tenderness, the richness and the straight-up deliciousness. It's a total solo act if you ask me – this vegetable is as close to Beyoncé as they come. Queen Eggplant, may she reign for ever. I'm fully aware that I'm not offering up a classic schnitzel here (in fact it's a cheat's version that avoids the egg and throws the crumb on top) but for this one-pan-wonder it made sense to pare back the steps to get you to tasty-town asap. And as an added bonus, the sourdough gets to be both crisp and swimming in sauce. I mean what's not to love?

effort 3/5 · veg · serves 4 · prep 10 min · cook 25 min

2 eggplants, sliced 1cm thick rounds crossways
2 tsp flaky salt
½ cup (75g) plain flour
½ cup (125ml) oil (I used a mix of olive and veg oil), plus 2 tbsp extra to drizzle
3 garlic cloves, thinly sliced
handful basil leaves, plus extra to serve
400g can chopped tomatoes
150g grated mozzarella
100g pitted olives, sliced
50g thinly sliced prosciutto
250g sourdough, torn into pieces
250g buffalo mozzarella, torn

Toss eggplant and salt in a colander and stand to soften for at least 1 hour. Toss in flour and shake to remove excess.

Heat oil in a frypan over medium-high heat. Working in batches, add eggplant pieces and fry, turning halfway, for 2–3 minutes, or until golden. Transfer to a baking dish, arraning to edges, and continue with the remaining pieces. Keep oil in pan.

Preheat oven to 200°C fan forced.

Add garlic and basil to remaining cooking oil and cook until golden. Add tomatoes and a half can-full of water (I use it to wash the can out). Bring to the boil then pour over the eggplant in the baking dish. Scatter with grated mozzarella, olives, prosciutto, torn bread and buffallo mozzerella, then drizzle with extra oil.

Bake for 15–20 minutes, or until golden. Scatter with extra basil leaves.

prep ahead

Once fried and topped with tomato sauce and crumb, you could have this parmi ready and waiting in the fridge for when you're ready to serve. It will keep there for up to 4 days prebake!

no fry

If you want to avoid the frying in oil, feel free to bake the slices of eggplant on a rack with a spray of oil for 20 minutes, turning halfway, or until tender and cooked through.

PIZZA

Cheese + dough + toppings = endless possibilities. Pizza will always be my kryptonite. It has me weak at the knees but strong in the hands so I can grab it and eat it.

SLAP IT TOGETHER

tandoori pizza
on naan
(pg 218)

GO TO

pesto margi
pan pizza
(pg 222)

LONG GAME

deep-dish
pepperoni pizza
(pg 224)

tandoori pizza on naan

These pizzas are pretty unorthodox. No tomato, no tomato sauce – but don't worry, there's still cheese (thank god for that). Using the store-bought garlic naan is the ultimate cheat if you ask me. Feel free to keep them as a base and go a little more traditional with your toppings. But before you do, try these, because you might just be a convert. It's the mint yoghurt for me that freshens everything up and brings these pizzas to life.

 effort 1/5 veg serves 4 prep 10 min cook 10 min

4 frozen garlic naan*, thawed
⅓ cup (90g) tandoori paste*
100g mozzarella, coarsely grated
1 cup (160g) shredded cooked chicken
  or tandoori chicken
1 red onion, thinly sliced
1 bunch broccolini, thinly sliced
2 tbsp mint chutney*, thawed
½ cup (140g) thick Greek-style yoghurt
juice of ½ lemon
rocket leaves, to serve

Specialty ingredients
Frozen naan and mint chutney can be
found in the freezer at Indian grocers.
Grab the tandoori paste while you're
there.

Preheat oven to 200°C fan forced. Grease and line 2 baking trays with baking paper.

Place naan on trays and divide the paste among them, spreading out to edges. Scatter with mozzarella and top with chicken, onion and broccolini. Bake for 10 minutes, or until cheese is melted.

Combine chutney, yoghurt and lemon in a bowl and season to taste. Spoon over pizzas and finish with rocket leaves to serve.

 make it veg Sub the chicken for cooked potatoes and sliced paneer and finish with some chickpeas.

 use it up Any leftover roast meat goes well here. Lamb, chicken – even roast pumpkin!

SELF-RAISING FLOUR

PESTO

YOGHURT

THE EASIEST PIZZA DOUGH

There are three secret ingredients to a successful cheat pizza dough: stability (SR flour); reliability (yoghurt); flavour (pesto). Their powers combined and you've got yourself a fluffy crisp pizza base you will want to write home about — and by that, I just mean text a friend. Turn the page for the pizza particulars (aka the recipe).

3-INGREDIENT PIZZA DOUGH STEP X STEP

1. Weigh out your self-raising flour, ice-cube pesto (page 132) and yoghurt.

2. Mixxy mixxy.

3. Combine and transfer to a clean work surface.

4. Divide into two.

5. Press out into an oiled ovenproof pan (we used a grill-pan, but any ovenproof frypan works).

6. Place over high heat for 2–3 minutes, or until base is golden.

7. Combine sauce ingredients.

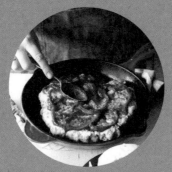

8. Add sauce ingredients to par-cooked crisp base.

9. Top with tomatoes, cheese and basil and bake.

pesto margi pan pizza

Flat bread dough–turned pizza dough–turned pan pizza. This recipe has gone full circle and has been given the full treatment. Three-ingredient, 5-minute dough – this is the recipe we all have the time for. Get your toppings and meet me at the stove! Using the flatbread recipe everyone loses their mind over, these pan pizzas get a crisp bottom before heading into a hot oven. Pizza in 15 minutes; surely that's quicker than takeway delivery! Also a total fan of delivered pizza though – no judgement here. See previous page for a step-by-step demo.

effort 2/5 · veg · serves 4 · prep 10 min · cook 30 min

⅓ cup (80ml) passata
1 tbsp tomato paste
3 garlic cloves, finely grated
1 tsp dried oregano
1 tsp porcini powder*
1 punnet cherry tomatoes
200g mozzarella cheese, sliced
1 bunch basil, leaves picked
2 tbsp olive oil, plus extra for drizzling
fresh burrata or buffalo mozzarella, torn,
 to serve (optional, but i mean...)

Dough
2⅓ cups (350g) self-raising flour
1½ cups (375g) thick Greek-style yoghurt
1 tbsp ice-cube pesto (page 132)
 or sub with store bought, plus
 extra to serve

Specialty ingredient
*Powdered, dried porcini mushrooms
adds a fantastic depth to sauces
because of its umaminess.*

Preheat oven to 220ºC fan forced.

For the dough, place all ingredients in a bowl and mix to combine. Divide into 2 and press out on a lightly floured work surface until you have 10cm-wide pieces. Drizzle an ovenproof frypan with 1 tablespoon of oil and add one piece of dough. Cook over medium high heat for 2–3 minutes, or until base is golden.

Combine passata, tomato paste, garlic, oregano and porcini powder in a bowl and season to taste. Spoon half over par-cooked crisp base and top with half the cherry tomatoes, cheese and a handful of the basil leaves, reserving some for garnish. Drizzle with half the oil and bake for 12 minutes or until cheese is golden and pizza is cooked through. Serve scattered with basil leaves, a drizzle of olive oil and burrata or torn fresh mozzarella, if using.

Repeat with remaining dough and toppings.

prep ahead
The pizza sauce for these is super handy to have on hand, make bulk and keep it in a jar in the fridge to whip out for speedy dinners.

jazz it up
Pump up the toppings for a make-your-own-pizza station: sliced mushrooms, olives, ham, pepperoni, capsicum, spinach leaves, red onion, or canned pineapple (controversial, I know).

deep-dish pepperoni pizza

Helping open a pizza place while in the first trimester of pregnancy was a true test of my pizza love. But it took this pizza to bring my cravings back to where they rightfully should have been from the get-go, and not in pickles and anchovies. It's the thick crust for me, and the slow fermentation – though it should be said you can use this dough for thin crust pizza also! Divide into 3 and press out to a round then pre-bake with tomato sauce before adding any toppings and baking once more for a crisp base every time!

effort 4/5 | serves 6–8 | prep 2 hr | cook 30 min | begin recipe 1–2 days ahead

polenta for dusting
¼ (60ml) cup olive oil, plus extra for drizzling
4 garlic cloves, thinly sliced
handful of basil leaves
2 x 400g cans crushed tomatoes
100g grated mozzarella
100g stracchino*
200g fresh mozzarella, torn
200g pepperoni or sliced salami
½ bunch oregano, leaves picked
grated Parmesan and oregano leaves, to serve

Tagglio dough
1 tsp dried yeast
2 tsp flaky salt
1 tsp diastatic malt* (optional)
2 cups (500ml) water
5 cups (750g) strong flour, plus extra for dusting
⅓ cup (80ml) extra virgin olive oil

*Specialty ingredients
Diastatic malt powder is a top secret with bread baking and enhances the texture and look of the dough. Found in health-food shops, it's optional but can make a big difference to the end result! Stracchino is a young cheese that tastes like the inside of a fresh mozzerella ball, and is spreadable. Feel free to sub with extra torn fresh mozzarella.

To make dough, combine yeast, salt, malt (if using), water and flour. Add 1 tablespoon of olive oil and mix to combine. Leave in a large non-reactive bowl for 1 hour at room temperature.

Fold dough over like a taco, drizzle with remaining oil, cover and chill in the fridge, for 1–2 days depending on how much you want it to ferment. If it has doubled in size by the first day, fold like a taco so it can make it to 2 days, but only if it's doubled in size. Leave it be if it hasn't.

Preheat oven to 220ºC fan forced. Grease a 20cm x 30cm shallow baking tray with oil and scatter with polenta.

Transfer dough to a lightly floured work surface. Press out with fingertips, edges first, then across the middle. Flip and repeat. Flip once more and press to fit the tray, pushing the dough up the sides to create a higher crust. Cover with a tea towel and stand for 30 minutes–1 hour to rise slightly and come to room temperature.

For the sauce, heat oil in a saucepan over medium-high heat. Add garlic and cook for 3–4 minutes, or until golden. Carefully (it may spit) add basil leaves and cook for a further 2 minutes, or until bubbles subside. Add canned tomatoes and bring to the boil, then remove from heat.

Spoon half the sauce over dough and bake for 15 minutes, or until dough is just cooked through but not too coloured. Scatter with some cheese, remaining sauce, pepperoni, then more cheese. Bake for a further 10 minutes or until cheese is melted and crust is golden.

Cut and serve scattered with Parmesan, oregano leaves and a drizzle of olive oil.

FRIT ME

These fritters are fierce little things. A batter stuffed to the brim with fruit or veg, pan-fried and served with condiments (always) – what a way to cook. These are quite literally screaming COOK ME. I hope you do.

SLAP IT TOGETHER

pear and banana fritters (pg 228)

GO TO

freezer fritters (pg 230)

LONG GAME

kimchi fritter with kewpie mayo and BBQ sauce (pg 232)

pear and banana fritters

These are my daughter Zoe's favourite. Because they have banana in them, but mostly because they're golden yellow and fluffy and resemble something close to bread (another favourite). These are our Sunday brekkie fritters, that make me happy with every bite.

effort 1/5 · veg · serves 4 · prep 10 min · cook 15 min

50g butter, plus extra for greasing
2 pears, coarsely grated (I used
   Packham pears)
1 banana, mashed
2 eggs
½ cup (125g) buttermilk or
   Greek-style yoghurt
1½ cups (225g) self-raising flour
zest and juice of 1 lemon
1 tsp vanilla bean paste
½ tsp baking powder
maple syrup, for drizzling

Spiced sugar
2 tbsp caster sugar
½ tsp ground cinnamon
pinch of ground cloves

Heat a non-stick frypan over low heat and melt butter. Transfer butter to a bowl with pear, banana, eggs, buttermilk, flour, zest, juice, vanilla bean paste and baking powder. Whisk to combine.

Combine spiced sugar ingredients.

Return greased pan to heat, working in batches, add tablespoons of batter to the pan and cook for 1–2 minutes each side, or until cooked through and golden. Transfer to a plate, scatter with sugar, and keep warm. Continue with the remaining batter, greasing between batches.

Serve fritters with maple syrup for drizzling and remaining spiced sugar.

spice it up
A little cocoa in these will add a point of difference if you're headed down that heavy rotation route, like me. It's like a whole different fritter.

use it up
Any fruit you can grate can go in here. A peach, apple, kiwifruit, strawberries, even blueberries. It's a batter to carry any and all fruits, even veggies if you want to pop some zucchini in there too.

freezer fritters

Corn fritters were a staple in our house growing up. Always served with tomato sauce, they were the thing to cook when you weren't super hungry, usually after days spent at grandparents' houses stuffing our faces. The crunch of the batter and sweetness of the corn, or peas if that's more your vibe, is a match made in heaven. The trick with these is adding the veg while its still frozen – gets things all sticky and keeps the batter cold.

effort 3/5	veg	serves 4	prep 5 min	cook 25 min

⅓ cup (30g) grated semi-soft cheese (I used Manchego, see bottom page for more options)
1 small zucchini, coarsely grated
½ cup (75g) self-raising flour
2 spring onions, thinly sliced
⅓ cup (80ml) milk
2 eggs, lightly whisked
2 cups (300g) frozen corn or peas
½ cup (125ml) vegetable oil to shallow fry
avocado slices, lemon wedges and tomato sauce, to serve

Place cheese, zucchini, flour, most of the spring onion (keep some of the green back for serving) in a bowl and toss to coat. Add milk, eggs and frozen veg and stir to combine. Mixture will seem quite thick and cakey! Season with salt and cracked pepper.

Heat oil in a frypan over medium heat. Add shallow quarter cups of fritter mix and cook, in batches, turning halfway, for 3–4 minutes, or until golden brown and cooked through. Transfer to a plate lined with a piece of paper towel to drain excess oil, and continue with remaining mixture.

Serve fritters scattered with remaining spring onion, avocado slices , lemon wedges and tomato sauce.

use it up
Any semi-soft cheese works in these. Throw in some halloumi, paneer, Tasty cheese or gruyère.

jazz it up
A poached egg and some bacon! Heat a tall saucepan or stock pot of water over high heat and bring to the boil. Add a good splash of vinegar. Reduce heat to low and swirl pan with a wooden spoon. Quickly crack eggs into the centre of the swirling water. Increase heat to medium and don't touch for 3 minutes. Good to go!

kimchi fritter
with kewpie mayo and bbq sauce

I would put kimchi in everything if I could. Kimchi mayo, kimchi toastie, kimchi noodles, kimchi dumplings. But this is a good start. Try this and tell me you too aren't hooked on all things kimchi. Based on the idea of a Japanese okonomiyaki, this fritter is packed with flavour. Yes this is a long game, but only cos it's a slightly fancier fritter. Other than that it's pretty FAST!

effort 2/5	veg	serves 4	prep 10 min	cook 15 min

2 eggs
1 cup (220g) kimchi*
¾ cup (180ml) water
1 cup (150g) self-raising flour
⅔ cup (100g) cornflour
350g white cabbage, shredded
   (approx. ¼ cabbage)
2 spring onions, sliced
vegetable oil, for shallow frying
Kewpie mayo, smoky BBQ sauce,
   lemon wedges, coriander leaves,
   toasted sesame seeds and
   sriracha*, to serve

*Specialty ingredient
Kimchi is a Korean side dish. One of the most common types is made by fermenting cabbage alongside garlic and chilli. Sriracha is a chilli sauce used to add a kick to a dish. Also called 'rooster sauce', cos of the rooster on the bottle.

Combine eggs, kimchi and water in a bowl. Add flours and mix well to combine. Fold through cabbage and most of the spring onion, keeping some for serving, and mix to coat.

Heat 1cm of oil in a large frypan over medium-low heat and, cooking in batches, add one-quarter of the mixture to pan. Use the back of the measuring spoon to spread out in the pan, to 1cm thick, and cook for 2–3 minutes, or until golden. Carefully flip and cook for a further 2–3 minutes, or until cooked through.

Transfer to a tray lined with paper towel and repeat with remaining mixture.

Drizzle with mayo and BBQ sauce, and serve with lemon wedges, sesame, remaining spring onion and sriracha.

---

 use it up Throw any veg you like in here – carrot, any kind of cabbage, zucchini, corn, peas, beans – you'll know when the batter has hit its limit.

 jazz it up Some chopped crispy pork belly (page 106) takes this up a notch and makes it a bit of a showstopper.

LOW & SLOW

I am a major fan of anything you can set and forget. Be it in the slow cooker, in a pot in the oven, or a plant that requires little to no attention in the garden but grows tall and covered in beautiful flowers . . . I'm still trying to find this plant so do let me know if it exists. I digress. Being slow cooked, these recipes are all long games I guess but still play to the 3-way approach with the scale of effort required. Enjoy slowly — if that's even possible.

SLAP IT TOGETHER
pulled chicken
nachos
(pg 236)

GO TO
beef osso buco
massaman with
quickles
(pg 238)

LONG GAME
slow-roasted lamb
shoulder with
preserved lemon
(pg 240)

pulled chicken nachos

Nachos are the thing you cook when eating not at the table. Whether it's summer and you're in the backyard, or your huddled around the TV watching sport, it's the meal to share and leave crumbs all over the floor. It's of course totally fine if you choose to have this at the table – I'm sure the crumb sitch is far more manageable there. Enjoy!

| effort 2/5 | gluten free | serves 4 with leftover chicken | prep 10 min | cook 2–3 hr |

200g natural salted corn chips
200g grated mozzarella cheese
1 small red onion, thinly sliced
½ cup sliced pickled jalapeños, finely
  chopped, plus 2 tbsp pickling liquid
shredded lettuce, coriander leaves, sour
  cream and hot sauce, to serve

Pulled chick
800g chicken breasts, slashed
  with the grain
1 orange, halved
2 x 400g cans whole tomatoes
400g can mixed beans
½ bunch oregano, leaves picked
2 tbsp tomato paste
2 tbsp chipotle sauce*
2 tbsp olive oil
2 tbsp smoked paprika
3 tsp each ground cumin, ground
  coriander and onion powder
pinch of allspice and garlic powder
1 tbsp brown sugar

Specialty ingredient
Chipotle is a Mexican chilli, and you can find chipotle sauce in a can with other specialty Mexican items in supermarkets or Mexican grocers. Alternatively, feel free to sub with ½–1 tsp (taste as you go) chipotle powder, which can sometimes be easier to find.

For the pulled chick, place everything in a slow cooker or heavy-based roasting pan and mix to combine. Cover and cook either in a 150°C fan forced oven for 2½ hours or for 4 hours on the high setting in the slow cooker, until the chicken is tender and pulls easily. Squeeze orange into cooking juices and shred chicken using 2 forks.

Preheat oven or grill to 200°C fan forced. Arrange corn chips on baking tray or ovenproof serving plates. Spoon over half of the chicken and scatter with cheese. Bake for 5–10 minutes, or until the cheese is melted.

Meanwhile, toss onion with jalapeño liquid and stand to quickle slightly.

To serve, scatter nachos with quickled onion, jalapeños, lettuce and coriander and serve with sour cream and hot sauce alongside for adding.

use
it up
Any cans of beans you want to get rid of should work in here. I'm all about using what you have and adapting the recipe to you, not the other way around.

more
veg
please
Some finely chopped capsicum in the chicken mix, a cup of frozen corn when you pull the chick and some sliced avocado to finish are some good veg options.

beef osso buco massaman
with quickles

A big bowl of curry fixes everything. This one, served with quickles (quick pickles), rice and roti, leaves no flavour page unturned. By using osso buco (cross-cut beef shank) and cooking it low and slow, we get the beautiful bone marrow to melt into the sauce and make it extra silky! (Licks lips.)

effort 4/5 · serves 4–6 · prep 15 min · cook 4–6 hr

½ cup (125g) massaman curry paste
2 tbsp crunchy peanut butter
5 garlic cloves, thinly sliced
2 French shallots, sliced
1kg beef osso buco
2 lemongrass stalks, base finely
  chopped
4 makrut lime leaves, bruised
800ml coconut cream
2 tbsp pomegranate molasses
1 cup (250ml) water
500g small cleaned waxy potatoes,
  halved
¼ cup (60ml) fish sauce
juice of 2 limes
2 tsp brown sugar
steamed rice, roti, pomegranate
  seeds (optional) and coriander
  leaves, to serve

Quickles
½ cup (125ml) white vinegar
2 tbsp caster sugar
3 star anise
8 radishes, quartered
½ cup (125ml) boiling water
1 Lebanese cucumber, thinly sliced
1 small red onion, thinly sliced
1 small red chillies, thinly sliced

Specialty ingredients
*Makrut lime leaves are from a makrut
lime plant and are aromatic and
citrussy. Found at Asian grocers with
the fruit and veg, they can be frozen
so grab a pack, use what you need
and freeze the remainder.*

Place massaman paste, peanut butter, garlic, shallot, beef, lemongrass, makrut lime leaves, coconut cream, pomegranate molasses and water in a heavy-based casserole pot or slow cooker and mix to combine. Cook covered in a 150°C fan forced oven or in a slow cooker set to high for 4–6 hours, or until meat is tender and falling off the bone. (Alternatively, set the slow cooker to low and cook overnight.)

Meanwhile, for the quickles, place vinegar, sugar, star anise and radishes in a heatproof bowl along with boiling water. Chill until required.

Place potatoes in a saucepan, cover with cold water and place over high heat. Bring to the boil and cook for 15 minutes, or until tender, then drain.

When meat is cooked and you're ready to serve, add cucumber, onion and chilli to pickle. Stir fish sauce, lime juice, sugar and cooked potatoes through curry and season to taste.

Serve curry with rice, roti, pomegranate seeds (if using), coriander leaves and quickles.

slow-roasted lamb shoulder
with preserved lemon

My go-to when I have a big group of people coming over is a slow-cooked shoulder of lamb. It's effortless in the way it's cooked and the result is always exceptional. The marinade for this lamb can also be used for chicken or even fish. The onion and lemon do this cool thing where they tenderise the meat slightly, and when charred at the end it all blisters into deliciousness.

 effort 3/5   gluten free   serves 6–8   prep 30 mins + marinating   cook 6–8 hr   begin recipe 1 day ahead

1 bone-in lamb shoulder
2 cups (500ml) chicken stock
½ cup (125ml) white wine
400g cleaned waxy or all-rounder
   potatoes, sliced 5mm thin
2 cups (500g) mixed marinated olives
1 lemon, sliced and cut into 2cm
   pieces
1 bunch mint, leaves picked, most
   finely shredded
⅓ cup (80ml) malt vinegar
1 tsp brown sugar
¼ cup (60ml) boiling water

Lamb marinade
1 small red onion
4 cloves garlic
50g preserved lemon*
2 tsp dried oregano
¼ cup (60ml) extra virgin olive oil

*Specialty ingredients
Preserved lemon can be found in a jar at most good delis. Preserved with salt, it gives a really different lemon profile to a dish. I like to use the rind and salty flesh, although this isn't common.

For the marinade, place all ingredients in a small food processor or blender and whiz until smooth. Massage mixture all over the lamb shoulder in a roasting pan and marinate overnight.

Preheat oven to 150°C fan forced.

Add the stock and wine to lamb and cover with foil. Roast for 6–8 hours, or until meat is falling off the bone.

Increase oven to 180°C fan forced. Remove foil and add potatoes, olives and lemon pieces and roast for a further 20–25 minutes, or until lamb is golden and potatoes are cooked through.

Combine shredded mint, malt vinegar, sugar and boiling water in a bowl and season to taste. Spoon some over the lamb and serve scattered with mint leaves and remaining sauce alongside.

---

 m8s with   The maple roasted pumpkin and couscous salad with raisin dressing (page 186) and kaley no-mayo warm slaw (page 178).

 prep ahead   When I find lamb shoulder for a good price, I like to marinate and freeze the lamb in a snap-lock bag. That way I can pull it out and it's ready to hit the oven when I have the reason (and people) for cooking it!

BAKING 101

Bake with the confidence of a three-year-old dressed in a superhero outfit. Cos if these recipes don't fly, I don't know what will. Here's some tips for getting there:

Growing up with dinners at my grandparents' house, there was never not sweets. Even if it was just some canned fruit and ice cream or a baked lemon delicious, there would always be something. I'd say this love for baking started here, then got catapulted by my own mum who studied patisserie when I was a teenager and brought home profiteroles and panforte. So when I have sweets, they have got to be full of flavour.

I'll always go all in. I wanted to include sweets in this book because 1. yum; 2. it seems baking gets a rap for being hard and maximum fuss. But it need not be – it can totally be simple and easy.

Theses recipe are great building blocks for sweets that really hit the taste buds and get you baking at home. Some are as simple as needing a bowl and spoon to mix them together and others drag in a few electrical appliances, but I'll only use it if I think it's super necessary.

I just have one rule when it comes to baking: MEASURE! Whether with scales or cup measurements, make sure to weigh your way through.

SPOILER ALERT, AUSSIES!

When it comes to tablespoons, in Australia, a standard tablespoon measure is 20ml, or 4 teaspoons. In the US, UK and New Zealand, however, a tablespoon holds 15ml, or 3 teaspoons. Where it will make a huge difference in the recipes, I have used teaspoon measures instead of tablespoons to be safe and to be sure you get the right amount.

TO BRING THE GF

Gluten-free flour has come a long way in the past five years. So I can confidently suggest easily interchanging the flours where necessary to make your baking gluten-free friendly. I have to say I'm a major fan of gluten-free flours that contain multiple flours like potato, rice and millet. I find if there's more than one they carry each other's weaknesses to get the job done.

MY BAKING MUST-HAVES
- decent choc chips
- vanilla paste and extract
- condensed milk
- butter
- milk powder
- free-range eggs
- buttermilk
- scales

 **Hawt tip!**

Isn't it the worst when you run out of self-raising flour?

1 cup (150g) plain flour 1½ tsp baking powder and a pinch of bicarb 1 cup self-raising flour.

CRUM-BLE

Let's get rrrrready to CRUMMMMBLE! Eat the crumble, taste the crumble, be the crumble. Fruit and crunch — what can go wrong? Well, nothing — all things can only go right when there's crumble. Also, crumble usually means ice cream, and I mean . . . yum.

SLAP IT TOGETHER

fruit plate crumble (pg 246)

GO TO

sticky lemon crumble pie (pg 248)

LONG GAME

deep-dish apple cobbler crumble (pg 250)

fruit plate crumble

This recipe makes use of the freezer. After making a bulk crumb and storing it in the freezer, it's just a matter of cutting some off and popping it on top of the fruit before it hits the oven. Convenience is king when it comes to this crumble.

effort 2/5   veg   serves 4   prep 15 min   cook 20 min

500g fruit of choice, fresh, frozen or
   tinned (I went for a combo of frozen
   strawberries, cherries, blueberries
   and canned apricots)
⅓ cup (80g) firmly packed brown
   sugar
¼ cup (60ml) triple sec, or sub
   with fruit juice
1 sprig rosemary
cream, yoghurt or ice cream to serve

Bulk crumble mixture
250g butter, melted
1¼ cup (300g) firmly packed
 brown sugar
1⅓ cup (200g) plain flour
1 cup (100g) shredded coconut
1 cup (100g) rolled oats
pinch of flaky salt

Preheat oven to 200°C fan forced.

Toss fruit, sugar, triple sec and rosemary in bowl and leave to stand and macerate for 5–10 minutes while you prepare the crumble.

For the crumble, combine all ingredients in a bowl.

Divide fruit mixture among 4 shallow ovenproof plates (I used enamel) or 1 large 3-cup capacity baking dish. Scatter enough crumble to just cover your fruit, then freeze remaining crumble mix either as one piece to cut from or in separate containers or snap lock bags for future use.

Bake fruit crumbles for 20–30 minutes, or until golden and bubbling and fruit has softened. Serve with cream, yoghurt or ice cream.

make it vegan

Sub the butter for coconut oil or vegan spread, and serve with vegan ice cream or coconut yoghurt.

spice it up

Spice the crumb with some cinnamon, allspice or cloves, or throw in some chopped nuts like pistachios and pecans. This is a great way of using up the end bit in a bag at the back of the freezer (where all loose end bits of nut bags should live).

sticky lemon crumble pie

I'm fully aware that this is pushing the boundaries of a crumble. But I thought you deserved something where the crumble was upside down. An upside-down pie crumble you can scoop into. This would have to be my version of a 'crack pie', a la Christina Tosi from Milk Bar. A pretzel crust, a tangy lemon filling and a brûlée top. Delicious! You'll need a blow torch to attain true crack status, but feel free to skip that step and scoop right in if you don't have one.

 effort 3/5   veg   serves 6–8   prep 10 min   cook 45 min

150g store-bought salted pretzels
¼ cup (35g) plain flour
150g unsalted butter, melted
1 lemon, thinly sliced
⅓ cup (75g) caster sugar, plus
   2 tbsp extra for brûlée
3 egg yolks
200g (½ a can) sweetened
   condensed milk
finely grated zest and juice of
   3 lemons, to get ½ cup lemon juice
¼ cup (60ml) cream, plus extra
   to serve

Preheat oven to 170°C fan forced. Grease and line a baking tray with baking paper.

To make the crumb base, place pretzels in a food processor and whiz until finely chopped. Add flour and butter and whiz again until mixture starts to clump together. Press crumb mixture into the base and sides of a 20cm tart or pie dish. Chill for 10 minutes to firm up slightly.

Toss lemon slices with 1 tbsp sugar. Arrange to one side of the baking tray.

Combine egg yolks, condensed milk, lemon zest and juice, cream and remaining sugar and pour over base. Reduce oven to 140°C and bake on tray next to lemon slices for 40–45 minutes or until filling is bubbling on the surface but still wobbles when given a slight shake and lemon slices have caramelised. Stand for 20 minutes to cool then chill to set, or keep going with the recipe and serve warm.

When you're ready to serve, scatter filling with extra sugar. Use a blow torch to caramelise the top, working from the centre out, tilting the melting sugar as you go to get an even toffee coating (aka brûlée). Arrange the caramelised lemons on the top and serve with a spoon to crack and scoop into.

 spice it up

Some dehydrated passionfruit powder in the pretzel crumb is a great way of bringing another layer of flavour.

 jazz it up

Ditch the brûlée and pile on a Swiss meringue. Combine 4 egg whites + 1 cup caster sugar and a pinch of creme of tartar. Place in a heatproof bowl over a saucepan of simmering water and cook, stirring, until mixture is hot and sugar dissolves. Transfer to a stand mixer and whisk on high until tripled in size and fluffy. Spoon over the top and torch.

deep-dish apple cobbler crumble

This deep-dish apple cobbler is layered with flavours. The spices in the apple, the tahini coating the filling, the pistachios and rose water in the crumb, the melting ice cream, the yum . . . yes, that is a flavour. I would happily eat this any day of the week if someone could be so kind as to peel and core all the apples. I haven't figured out a hack for that yet. Get the family involved? I did for this one.

effort 4/5 · veg · serves 6–8 · prep 30 min · cook 1½ hr

50g butter, chopped
1.4kg (approx. 8) Granny Smith
    apples, peeled, cored and chopped
    into 2cm pieces
¼ cup (60ml) golden syrup
finely grated zest and juice of 1 lemon
1 tbsp tahini
1 tbsp ground cinnamon
½ tsp ground cloves
ice cream, to serve

Cobbler crumb
200g butter, chopped
2 cups (300g) self-raising flour
1 tbsp pistachios, chopped, plus extra
    to serve
½ cup (125g) firmly packed
    brown sugar
½ cup (110g) caster sugar
2 tsp rose water*
1 tsp vanilla bean paste
1 tsp flaky salt
½ cup (125ml) boiling water

Specialty ingredient
*A flavoured water made from rose
petals. The best ones are found in
Middle Eastern grocers.*

Preheat oven to 160°C fan forced.

Place butter, apples, golden syrup, lemon zest and juice, tahini, cinnamon and cloves in a 2.5 litre capacity baking dish and cover with foil. Bake for 45–50 minutes, or until fruit is softened and cooked through.

Increase oven to 180°C fan forced.

For the crumb, place butter, flour, pistachio, sugars, rose water, vanilla and salt in the bowl of a food processor and whiz until a crumb forms. Add boiling water and whiz once more to form a smooth paste. Spoon over apple mixture and roughly cover (mixture will spread as it cooks). Bake for 45 minutes, or until golden and puffed.

Scatter with extra pistachios and serve with ice cream.

make it vegan Sub the butter for Nuttelex and swap the ice cream for a vegan substitute.

prep ahead The apple mixture can be made way ahead of time, making the cobbler addition a 5-minute job!

SLICE

Slices are a mirage: we cut them into small pieces as if to say that obviously that's the portion size. But we're never going to stop at one piece! These slices hit home-runs on flavour with simple execution.

SLAP IT TOGETHER

splice slice
(pg 254)

GO TO

fruit and nut brownie
(pg 256)

LONG GAME

banana caramel slice
(pg 258)

splice slice

Summer is sorted with these splice slice waffle crust bars — yep, that's about as much of a mouthful as these splice bars are. Lemon sorbet and vanilla ice cream is a winning combo here, and since I'm not asking you to make the ice cream? Well, sit back and enjoy! It basically makes itself, and once frozen it's ready to go. Ultimate birthday cake too, if you ask me — Luke are you reading this?!

effort 2/5 | veg | serves 12 | prep 45 min | make recipe 1 day ahead

2 cups (500g) lemon sorbet
2 cups (500g) vanilla ice cream
100g butter
2 tbsp golden syrup
1 tsp vanilla essence
170g store-bought waffle cones
¾ cup (180ml) pineapple juice
finely grated zest of 1 lemon, plus
 extra to serve (optional)

Line the base and sides of a 20cm x 30cm slice pan with baking paper, making sure you have enough overhang to help remove the slice once frozen.

Remove both sorbet and ice cream from the freezer and stand until required to soften.

Place butter, golden syrup and vanilla in a saucepan over high heat and cook for 3–4 minutes, or until butter has melted and mixture has come to the boil.

Whiz waffle cones in a food processor until finely chopped. Add syrup mixture and whiz to combine. Use half to line the base of the slice pan, pressing with the back of a spoon to smooth out as best you can.

Combine sorbet with pineapple juice and lemon zest in a bowl and pour over base. Freeze for 30 minutes, or until firm to touch. Spoon over ice cream and use a spatula to smooth over the top. Scatter with remaining waffle mixture and freeze for 4 hours or overnight, until firm.

Cut and serve scattered with extra lemon zest.

jazz it up
Wrap these bars with fancy paper and string and they make the cutest little ice-cream sandwiches. A fun treat at a birthday party!

prep ahead
Wrapped in something airtight, these will last in the freezer for 1–2 months.

fruit and nut brownie

Look, I'm a plain block of chocolate gal myself, but these fruit and nut brownies are enough to sway me. Especially because you can throw whatever you like in them. They are super-fudgy bites you will want to keep eating.

 effort 2/5 veg serves 12 prep 10 min cook 25 min

125g butter
125g dark chocolate
⅔ cup (150g) caster sugar
2 large eggs
1 tsp vanilla bean paste
2 tbsp cocoa powder, plus extra
   to dust
½ cup (75g) plain flour
¼ tsp flaky salt
½ tsp baking powder
200g fruits and nuts or even extra
   choc chips (I used prunes, golden
   raisins, walnuts and frozen cherries)

Preheat oven to 160°C fan forced. Grease and line the base and sides of a 20cm x 20cm brownie pan.

Melt butter and chocolate in a microwave-safe bowl in 20 second-bursts until the butter is melted. Stir to melt chocolate and combine into a smooth mixture. Add sugar and stir to dissolve. Add eggs one by one, mixing to incorporate. Add vanilla, cocoa, flour, salt and baking powder and mix to form a smooth batter. Fold through fruit and nuts of your choice.

Pour into prepared pan and smooth out. Bake for 25 minutes or until crisp on top.

Stand to cool, then chill for 1 hour to firm up. Cut and serve dusted with extra cocoa.

 use it up — This is a great one for using up dried fruit, nuts and remnants of choc chips from the pantry.

 prep ahead — Brownie can be made and stored in the freezer for up to 3 months.

banana caramel slice

Is there really anything I need to say to convince you to cook this? Other than the fact it has banana in it, so it's essentially a fruit salad – as my dear friend Warren Mendes would say. Also should be said, caramel slice freezes like a dream! A life hack I learnt from a young age, thanks to my Grandma who always had it on-hand in the freezer.

 effort 3/5 veg serves 12 prep 30 min cook 30 min

150g malt or shortbread biscuits
50g butter, melted
2 bananas, 1 whole, 1 thinly sliced
395g can sweetened condensed milk
¼ cup (60ml) golden syrup
70g butter, chopped
pinch of flaky salt
100g dark chocolate, melted
3 tsp vegetable oil

Preheat oven to 180°C fan forced. Grease and line the base and sides of a 12cm x 24cm loaf pan with baking paper.

To make the base, whiz biscuits, melted butter and one whole banana in a food processor. Transfer to prepared loaf pan and push with the back of a spoon to smooth out. Layer over sliced banana evenly.

Bake for 10 minutes, or until golden and firm to touch.

Meanwhile, place condensed milk, golden syrup, chopped butter and salt in a saucepan over medium heat. Cook, stirring, for 5 minutes or until combined and golden. Pour over baked base and return to the oven for 15–20 minutes, or until golden on top and bubbling. Combine chocolate and oil and pour over hot caramel. Smooth over with a small palette knife and stand at room temperature to cool. Chill for 2 hours or until firm.

Cut and serve.

 m8s with — Everyone – literally every page in this book wants to be friends with this slice.

 spice it up — A pinch each of cinnamon and nutmeg in the base can get people talking.

 use it up — Old bananas can go in here. Keep them in the freezer so they're on hand for exactly this sort of sitch.

MUFFIN

You must be the muffin woman – why yes, yes, I am. These are the things I end up cooking at around 2pm on a Sunday cos I'm 'bored' and end up eating three of with lashings of butter and then – spoiler – don't have room for dinner! Bizarre #wortheverymuffin

SLAP IT TOGETHER
sumac-spiced
blueberry muffins
(pg 262)

GO TO
savoury pumpkin
texas muffins
(pg 264)

LONG GAME
scruffins
(scroll x muffin)
(pg 266)

sumac-spiced blueberry muffins

It's the sumac in these that takes them from a standard blueberry muffin to a spiced goddess of fluffy muffin dreams. The citrus note it hits and keeps even post-bake is an incredible feat. Trust me on this one, you will start using sumac in all your baking after this. Sumac croissant?

 effort 2/5   veg   makes 12   prep 10 min cook 25 min

2 cups (300g) self-raising flour
1 cup (220g) caster sugar
½ tsp baking powder
1 tsp sumac*
½ tsp each ground cinnamon and
    mixed spice
50g butter, chopped
½ cup (125ml) buttermilk
2 eggs
1 tsp vanilla bean paste or extract
⅓ cup (80ml) vegetable oil
¼ cup (60ml) water
200g frozen blueberries
a good smattering of icing sugar for
    dusting, to serve

Specialty ingredient
Sumac, made from dried berries, is a tiny spice with huge flavour. With big citrus notes, it's one of my favourite spices to use if you're looking to add some tang.

Preheat oven to 180°C fan forced. Line a muffin pan with muffin cases.

Place the flour, sugar, baking powder, spices and butter in a wide bowl and use fingertips to smooch into the flour and create a breadcrumb texture. It's okay to have some bigger chunks. Add buttermilk, eggs, vanilla, oil and water and mix to combine. Fold through blueberries. Divide among muffin cases and bake for 25 minutes, or until cooked through and browned.

Cool in pan for 10 minutes before turning out.

Dust with icing sugar and serve warm.

 jazz it up Pour into a loaf pan and bake for an extra 20–25 minutes, or until cooked through. Drizzle with icing sugar mixed with a touch of lemon juice for a tea cake.

 use it up Throw any frozen berry in here or ditch the berries all together and throw in some choc chips.

savoury pumpkin texas muffins

Savoury muffins are the Trojan horse of the muffin world. They look like a muffin, are shaped like a muffin, but are full to the brim with cheese. The ultimate way to attack somebody's taste buds; these do not disappoint. My savoury muffins are packed with quite a decent amount of veg, too. So, you're welcome!

 effort 2/5
 veg
 makes 6
 prep 15 min
cook 25 min

spray oil
¾ cup (180ml) buttermilk
2 eggs
½ cup (100g) chopped sundried tomatoes
½ cup (125ml) vegetable oil
1 tbsp wholegrain mustard
1 tbsp onion relish
1 cup (125g) coarsely grated pumpkin
2 cups (50g) baby spinach leaves
100g ricotta
2 cups (300g) self-raising flour
½ tsp baking powder
6 cherry bocconcini
handful of sage leaves
butter, to serve

Preheat oven to 170°C fan forced. Spray a 6-hole non-stick Texas muffin pan with oil or line with large muffin cases.

Combine buttermilk, eggs, sundried tomato, oil, mustard, relish, pumpkin, spinach and ricotta in a bowl. Add flour and baking powder and mix to combine. Divide among muffin holes and push bocconcini into the middle of each muffin. Scatter with sage leaves and spray with oil and bake for 30-35 minutes, or until golden and cooked through. Cool in pan.

Serve with lashings of butter.

 jazz it up — A fried egg with one of these is a damn fine brekkie.

 use it up — Any ends of cheese can be coarsely grated and added.

 meat lovers — Some finely sliced ham thrown in the mixture is a winner for me.

scruffins (scroll x muffin)

Before you get angry at me, I'm getting you to start these one day in advance to make it easier. Trust me, this means the work happens as it sits in the fridge and chills overnight. The next morning it's a quick knock back, butter splash, spice dust, roll and cut and then they're sitting all over again for two hours to come to room temp. Perfect timing for morning tea. The active prep involved in these is actually quite minimal. It's about cooking smart, not hard, remember! Also, the citric acid in the icing makes it taste like sherbet!

 effort 4/5 veg makes 12 prep 2¼ hr cook 25 min begin recipe 1 day ahead

⅓ cup (80g) firmly packed brown sugar
2 tbsp ground cinnamon
2 tsp ground cardamom
50g butter, melted
1 cup (120g) icing sugar
¼ tsp citric acid
2–3 tbsp milk

Dough
1¼ cups (310ml) lukewarm milk
½ cup (110g) caster sugar
1½ tsp dried yeast
1 egg
150g butter, melted
4 cups (600g) plain flour
⅓ cup (50g) milk powder

For the dough, combine the lukewarm milk, caster sugar and yeast in the bowl of a stand mixer or a large bowl. Stand for 5 minutes without mixing until the yeast dissolves. Add remaining ingredients and mix with the dough hook for 6–8 minutes, or until the dough forms a smooth ball. Alternatively, knead with your hands – but this can take a little bit longer.

Roll out the dough to a 1cm thick rectangle (roughly 32cm x 22cm). Place on a baking tray and cover with cling film or a damp tea towel. Chill for 12 hours or overnight.

The next day, line a muffin tray with muffin cases. Combine brown sugar, cinnamon and cardamom.

Brush dough slab with melted butter and sprinkle a layer of sugar mixture across dough evenly. Carefully roll up from one of the the long sides to create a tight sausage then cut into 12 and add to muffin cases, spiral facing up. Cover and set aside in a warm place for 2 hours, to reach room temperature.

Preheat the oven to 190°C fan forced. Add a splash of water to the bottom of the oven, to create steam.

Bake the scruffins for 20–25 minutes, or until golden, risen and cooked through. Stand for 15 minutes to cool slightly. Combine icing sugar, citric acid and milk in a bowl, adding extra as needed to get the right consistency. Spoon over scruffins, and serve warm (this is non-negotiable – always serve warm).

 use it up
If you've got an old lonely apple or two in need of a home, feel free to coarsely grate him and scatter him across the dough before you roll it up and cut it. Apple scruffins are the next best thing to scruffins.

 prep ahead
The dough can chill in the fridge for up to 24 hours, just keep an eye on how it rises, and knock it back with a rolling pin if it gets out of control – and by that, I mean it doubles in size.

COO-KIE

Fact*: most burns in domestic kitchens come from trying to eat cookies straight out of the oven. These cookies, both round and square, are the ultimate starting block for filling your pantry with baked cookie goods – honestly, I wouldn't even bother putting them in a jar: they won't last that long. (*not a fact but should be)

SLAP IT TOGETHER
oaty ginger tray cookies
with milk icing
(pg 270)

GO TO
the cccs aka
choc chip cookies
(pg 274)

LONG GAME
jaffa brookies
(pg 276)

oaty ginger tray cookies
with milk icing

These are my tray cookies, where you make the dough, press it out, bake it then cut it – now if that's not a slap it together I don't know what is. And the ginger in the cookie? Well it turns up the heat on a traditional Anzac biscuit, that's for sure, and makes these cookies rather ginge' ius.

 effort 2/5 veg makes 12 prep 10 min cook 15 min

1½ cups (150g) rolled oats
1 cup (100g) shredded coconut
1 cup (150g) plain flour, sifted
1 cup (250g) firmly packed
  brown sugar
pinch of flaky salt
125g butter, melted
¼ cup (60ml) golden syrup
1½ tbsp ground ginger
¼ cup (60ml) water
½ tsp bicarb soda

Icing
1 cup (120g) icing sugar
1 tsp mixed spice
1–2 tbsp milk

Preheat oven to 180°C fan forced. Grease and line a baking tray with baking paper.

Combine oats, coconut, flour, sugar and salt in a large bowl. Place butter, golden syrup, ginger and water in a small saucepan over medium heat and cook for 2–3 minutes, or until melted and combined. Add bicarb soda carefully as the mixture will bubble and froth. Add to flour mixture and mix to combine.

Transfer to the prepared tray and press out until 6mm thick (use wet hands to make this easier).

Bake for 15 minutes, or until golden. Cut into 12 pieces while warm with a sharp knife. Stand to cool completely on tray.

Meanwhile, for the icing, combine icing sugar and mixed spice in a bowl. Add milk a bit at a time until you get the right consistency. Drizzle with a spoon over biscuits, or transfer to a piping bag or snap lock bag with the corner cut and squeeze over the top of the cooled biscuits. Stand to set then serve.

 jazz it up — Scatter chopped raisins and cranberries over the icing before it sets for a bark-like look.

 spice it up — Ditch the ginger and throw in ¼ cup raisins and 2 tsp mixed spice for a raisin toast vibe.

Just dough it (Nike, lets chat). Simple steps, not simple cookies (super-amazing cookies, actually) . . .

1. Partially melt the butter so it's sitting between melted and soft. Add sugars and mix to combine.

2. Add eggs one by one, mixing between additions.

3. Mixxy mixxy.

7. Mix and season with salt.

8. Transfer to a sheet of baking paper and shape into a log.

9. Roll to enclose like a Christmas bon bon and freeze to firm up.

EXIT

. . . turn the page for the recipe for getting this choc chip cookie (aka CCC) done. Just dough it — just COOK ME.

4. Add dry ingredients and vanilla.

5. Roughly mix to combine.

6. Fold through choc chips.

10. Slice into thick rounds.

11. Re-shape and neaten cookies using hands.

12. Boom. Ready to bake.

the cccs aka choc chip cookies

I love this recipe cos all you need is a bowl and spoon. No big stand mixer required, which is exactly what you want when you're craving cookies asap. Make sure to not skimp on the quality of the choc chips, they're kind of a game changer to these tasting insanely delicious or just delicious — and I know which one I'd prefer. For a bigger chew factor ditch the brown sugar for caster and bake the cookies for 8 minutes so the edges are cooked but the centre is still moist. Cool on trays and they should be firm enough to pick up. See previous page for a step-by-step demo.

effort 2/5	veg	makes 10-12	prep 30 min	cook 12 min

150g unsalted butter, chopped
½ cup (125g) firmly packed
   brown sugar
2 tbsp caster sugar
1 egg
2 tsp vanilla extract or paste
1½ cups (225g) plain flour
¼ cup (50g) milk powder*
1 tsp flaky salt
½ tsp baking powder
¼ tsp bicarb
200g good-quality dark
   chocolate chips

*Specialty ingredient
Milk powder is a great softener in baking, and it makes these cookies super crumbly.

Place butter and sugars in a microwave-safe bowl and cook on high for 30 seconds to soften and partially melt. Mix to combine. Add egg and whisk to combine. Add remaining ingredients and use hands or a large spoon to mix and combine into a dough. Transfer to a large piece of baking paper and roll to form a log. Chill for 1 hour or until firm.

Preheat oven to 180°C fan forced. Line 2 baking trays with baking paper.

Cut into 1–2cm thick rounds and place on prepared trays, spaced 3cm apart. Bake for 10–12 minutes, or until lightly golden and still soft.

Cool on trays to crisp. These will keep in an airtight container for up to 2 weeks (if they don't get eaten immediately).

jazz it up
Go choc on choc. Combine 1½ tbsp cocoa with 2 tbsp milk and add to the mix. Go for white, milk and dark chocolate chips. Boom.

use it up
A few nuts or some raisins and oats can be a great way of getting rid of a few pantry items.

jaffa brookies (brownie x cookie)

When I was growing up, Mum used to always make delicious cakes and brownies. She'd pull them out of the oven, and we'd all be so keen to grab a slice. Then she'd say something like 'Yeah they turned out nice – I added some orange essence to them', and we'd all exclaim 'WHYYYYYY?'. Well it turns out I've finally climbed onboard this fab combo, so this one's for you, Mum! xx

effort 4/5 · veg · makes 16 · prep 1¾ hr · cook 15 min

100g butter
150g 70% cocoa dark chocolate
2½ cups (300g) icing sugar
2 egg whites
1 whole egg
finely grated zest of 1 orange, plus
 extra to serve
1 tsp orange essence
½ tsp vanilla essence
⅓ cup (50g) self-raising flour
3 tsp cocoa powder
milk, to serve

Place butter and chocolate in a microwave-safe bowl and microwave in 20-second bursts until melted. Stir to combine.

Place sugar, egg whites, egg, orange zest and essences in a bowl and whisk briefly until sugar dissolves. Add chocolate mixture, flour and cocoa and mix to combine well. Chill mixture for 1 hour or overnight until firm and cold.

Preheat oven to 170°C fan forced and line 3 baking trays with baking paper.

Using heaped tablespoons to divide mixture, roll balls between wet hands. Return to the fridge to chill for 20 minutes, re roll and place onto prepared trays spaced 4cm apart.

Bake for 12–15 minutes, or until tops are shiny and cookies have spread. Scatter with extra orange zest. Cool on trays to crisp.

jazz it up — Pop a Jaffa in the centre of the balls before baking for the whole Jaffa experience.

use it up — Add the dregs from the bottom of the cornflake box to the mix. Finish with some melted choc and a walnut for something with crunch.

CHEESE-CAKE

Baked, set and whipped, these cakes put cheese first and we're totally on-board that train. TOOOT TOOOOT — the train is literally leaving, can you please hurry up?!

SLAP IT TOGETHER
cheesecake-stuffed brioche
(pg 280)

GO TO
cheesecake-misu
(pg 282)

LONG GAME
burnt butter basque cheesecake with aperol sauce
(pg 284)

cheesecake-stuffed brioche

'I can't believe they're not donuts', everyone will say as they chomp down on these cheesecake-stuffed bombs of deliciousness. It's truly a superior hack if you ask me. You'll find the buns near the hamburger buns, just avoid any with sesame seeds – but hey, it could make for some nice crunch.

effort 1/5 · veg · makes 12 · prep 10 min

250g cream cheese, softened
½ cup (100g) fresh ricotta
3 tsp vermouth or limoncello
3 tsp vanilla extract
finely grated zest of 1 lemon
½ cup (60g) icing sugar
2 tsp ground cinnamon
12 small brioche buns/sliders
¼ cup (30g) pistachios, ground
  or finely chopped

For the filling, place cream cheese, ricotta, vermouth or limoncello, vanilla, lemon zest and half of the icing sugar in the bowl of a food processor and whiz until thickened slightly.

Combine cinnamon and remaining icing sugar in a bowl.

Use a knife to cut buns three-quarters of the way through. Spoon or pipe in filling so that it is 2cm thick. Press to close, then roll filling side in pistachios. Dust with cinnamon sugar and serve.

 jazz it up If you're not a fan of outsourcing the bun, a choux pastry piped as profiteroles and baked would be a fab way to show off this filling. Could even chocolate dip them, too!

 prep ahead The filling can be made in advance and chilled until you're ready to stuff and roll.

cheesecake-misu

It pains me to have added to the endless -misu dishes in this world. Why must we find a way to make everything be almost like tiramisu but never quite enough to fully qualify. But here I am calling this cheesecake-misu, because you know what? It totally is. And the Tim Tam base? Well, you'll just have to COOK ME and let me know what you think (obviously amazing). No-bake cheesecake eat your heart out.

effort 3/5 · veg · serves 8–12 · prep 10 min · begin recipe 1 day ahead

200g Tim Tams
50g unsalted butter, melted
¼ cup (60ml) water
3 tsp gelatine
500g cream cheese
1 cup (250ml) cream
100g caramelised or plain white
  chocolate, melted
⅓ cup (75g) icing sugar
60ml espresso coffee (or sub with
  1 tbsp instant coffee and 2 tbsp
  boiling water)
2 tbsp cocoa powder, plus extra
  to serve

Mascarpone cream
1 tsp vanilla bean paste
250g mascarpone
½ cup (125ml) cream
1 tbsp icing sugar

To make the base, place biscuits in a food processor and whiz until finely chopped. Add butter and whiz again until mixture starts to clump together. Press crumb mixture into base of a 10cm x 15cm loaf pan and smooth with the back of a spoon. Chill.

To make the coffee filling, place water in a microwave safe bowl. Scatter with gelatine and stand for 5 minutes to dissolve and absorb most of the water. Microwave for 20 seconds then stir until a smooth liquid. Place cream cheese, cream, melted chocolate, icing sugar, coffee and gelatine mixture in the bowl of a food processor and whiz until smooth. Pour over prepared base. Chill for 4 hours or overnight to set.

For the mascarpone cream, place vanilla, mascarpone, cream and icing sugar in the bowl of a stand mixer fitted with the whisk attachment and whisk until stiff peaks form. Spoon or pipe over set cheesecake and dust with cocoa to serve.

jazz it up — Some chocolate-covered coffee beans to finish and maybe a little caramel sauce is an excellent idea

use it up — Sub the Tim Tams for any biccy you want.

burnt butter basque cheesecake
with aperol sauce

Thanks to Spain, it's literally okay to burn the shizza out of your cheesecake. Also, this bounty of yum comes with a sauce spiked with one of my favourite alcohols, Aperol. It's a no-brainer. COOK ME.

 effort 3/5   veg   serves 12   prep 10 min, plus chilling   cook 55 min   begin recipe 1 day ahead

100g unsalted butter, chopped
750g cream cheese, brought to room temperature
250g mascarpone
1½ cups (330g) caster sugar
1½ tbsp vanilla bean paste
5 eggs
1 cup (250ml) cream
¼ cup (35g) of plain gluten-free flour, sifted
2 cups (300g) frozen raspberries
½ cup (125ml) maple syrup
finely grated zest and juice of 1 lemon
2 tbsp Aperol (optional)

Preheat the oven to 200°C fan forced. Grease and line the base and sides of a 23cm round spring-form cake pan with baking paper. Making sure the paper extends 2cm higher than the top of the tin. Set aside on a baking tray until required.

Place butter in a saucepan over medium high heat. Melt, then cook for a further 3–4 minutes, until foam subsides and you're left with a brown butter. Remove from heat and transfer to a food processor with the cream cheese, mascarpone, sugar and vanilla and whiz until smooth and creamy. Add eggs one at a time, pulsing between additions and ensuring each egg incorporates well before adding the next. Add the cream and sift in flour. Whiz until combined and smooth.

Pour the mixture into prepared pan. Reduce oven to 180°C and bake for 50 minutes or until dark on top with a slight wobble across the top of the cheesecake. Leave in oven with the door slightly ajar for 1 hour, then transfer to the fridge to cool completely for at least 4 hours or overnight, until the centre of the cheesecake is firm to touch.

Place raspberries, maple and lemon zest and juice in a saucepan and bring to the boil. Cook for 5 minutes to reduce slightly then stir through Aperol. Remove from heat.

Cut cheesecake and serve with Aperol sauce.

 spice it up   A pinch of chai spices, such as cardamom, cinnamon, ginger, clove and some finely grated star anise and voilà – chai cheesecake!

 use it up   Sub the raspberries for any frozen berries you have, or ditch the sauce completely and drizzle with melted dark chocolate sauce or caramel for something a little decadent.

CAKE

Whoever said 'You can't have your cake and eat it too' was a confusing person. I say cook these cakes and eat them, and they'll still be here for you to cook again soon.

SLAP IT TOGETHER

sprinkle cupcakes
(pg 288)

GO TO

choc cake
à la bundt
(pg 290)

LONG GAME

carrot slab cake with
cream cheese icing
(pg 292)

sprinkle cupcakes

These cupcakes were born to be stars. I mean just look at them, literally covered in sprinkles. I'm a total fan and you will be too when you realise how easy they are, topped with store-bought frosting. Well, we don't call it 'slap it' for nothing.

effort 2/5 • veg • makes 12 • prep 10 min • cook 18 min

1½ cups (225g) self-raising flour
½ cup (60g) icing sugar
¼ tsp baking powder
pinch of flaky salt
⅓ cup (80ml) vegetable oil
40g butter, melted
1 egg
1½ tsp vanilla extract
1 cup (250ml) evaporated milk
2 tbsp sprinkles, plus extra to serve
store-bought vanilla frosting, to serve

Preheat oven to 180°C fan forced. Line a muffin tray with 12 cupcake cases.

Combine flour, sugar, baking powder and salt in a bowl. Add oil, butter, egg, vanilla and half a cup evaporated milk and mix to combine. Add sprinkles and fold through briefly, taking care not to over-mix so they keep their colour. Divide evenly among cases.

Bake for 15–18 minutes, or until golden and risen. Use a skewer to poke 1–2 holes in cupcakes and brush with remaining evaporated milk. Stand to cool and soak in the milk.

Spoon frosting over cooled cakes, and shape with a butter knife. Scatter with sprinkles and serve.

m8s with
Considering these will probably be eaten at a party I suggest my fennel sausage rolls (page 40) and cheesy onion French stix (page 30) for an all-round party vibe.

use it up
Remaining evaporated milk can be used as a substitute for milk in any baking recipe if the majority is still standard cow's milk. So, keep what's left in the can.

choc cake à la bundt

There's a hole in this cake. But there doesn't have to be. The same batter can be popped into a 22cm cake pan and baked as a round if that's more your style. Regardless of shape, this cake is all you want from a moist (yep, I said it), rich chockie cake. Secret ingredients being the vinegar and espresso coffee – total game changers.

 effort 3/5 veg serves 12 prep 15 min cook 1 hr

spray oil
250g butter, softened
⅔ cup (190g) firmly packed brown sugar
¼ cup (55g) caster sugar
1 tsp vanilla
4 eggs
1⅓ cup (200g) plain flour
⅓ cup (50g) cocoa powder
2½ tsp baking powder
½ cup (150g) sweetened condensed milk
¼ cup (60ml) espresso coffee (or sub with 3 tsp instant dissolved in ¼ cup hot water)
¼ cup (60ml) milk
2 tsp white vinegar
½ tsp flaky salt, plus extra to serve

Choc ganache
200ml cream
¼ cup (75g) sweetened condensed milk
100g 70% cocoa dark chocolate, chopped

Preheat oven to 160°C fan forced. Grease a 25cm non-stick Bundt tin with spray oil.

Place butter, sugars and vanilla in a stand mixer fitted with the paddle attachment, or use hand beaters to beat until pale and sugar is mostly dissolved. Add eggs one at a time, combining as you go. Remove and fold in the remaining ingredients with a spatula. Spoon into prepared tin.

Bake for 50–55 minutes, or until a skewer inserted into the middle comes out clean. Stand to cool for 5 minutes then invert onto a cooling rack and cool.

Meanwhile, for the icing, heat cream and condensed milk in a small saucepan over high heat and bring to the boil. Remove from heat and add chocolate. Stand for 5 minutes to soften. Mix to combine until you reach a thick, smooth consistency. Pour over cake while still warm, scatter with extra salt and serve.

 spice it up Add 1 tsp Kashmiri chilli powder mixed with 1 tbsp miso paste to the batter to give this cake a real kick.

 use it up Any remaining condensed milk can be used to make a Vietnamese iced coffee! Drizzle into a glass and fill with ice then pour over some hot espresso.

carrot slab cake
with cream cheese icing

Carrot cake smothered in cream-cheese frosting is the ultimate send-off and finale to this book. It shows the balance of savoury and sweet, the restraint with luxuries when needed and the opulence when required (see the icing for this cake) and the need to always go big or go home. Maximum of flavour, minimum of fuss — unless the fuss is required, in which case make the fuss worth it. And trust me, it's worth it for this cake.

 effort 3/5 veg serves 12 prep 20 min cook 50 min begin recipe 1 day ahead

200g walnuts, chopped
½ cup (125ml) orange juice
400g (approx. 3) carrots, coarsely grated
3cm piece fresh turmeric, finely grated
1 cup (250g) firmly packed brown sugar
2 tsp each ground cinnamon and mixed spice
¾ cup (180ml) light olive oil
½ cup (125ml) thick Greek-style yoghurt
3 eggs
1 tsp vanilla bean paste
3 cups (450g) self-raising flour
½ tsp baking powder
2 tsp freeze-dried raspberry powder* (optional)

Cream cheese frosting
500g cream cheese
finely grated zest and juice of 1 lemon
75g butter, chopped and softened
1¼ cup (150g) icing sugar

Speciality ingredient
Freeze-dried raspberry powder can be found in cake-supply shops, specialty grocers and some supermarkets.

Soak walnuts in orange juice overnight.

Preheat oven to 160ºC fan forced. Grease and line the base and sides of a 22cm x 32cm x 5cm high cake tin or roasting tray.

Combine carrot, turmeric, sugar, spices, oil, yoghurt, eggs, vanilla and walnut mix in a bowl. Add flour and baking powder and mix well to combine. Transfer to prepared cake tin and bake for 45–50 minutes, or until a skewer inserted into the middle comes out with only crumbs. Stand to cool.

Meanwhile, for the cream cheese frosting, place everything in the bowl of a food processor and whiz until thick and smooth. Chill until required.

Spoon icing over the top of the cooled cake, spreading to the edges. Finish with freeze-dried raspberry (if using) to serve.

 jazz it up — I love it when carrot cake gets served with yoghurt. It might be a Kiwi thing? But the sourness really cuts through the sweetness of the cake and I'm a total fan.

 use it up — Feel free to throw in some grated zucchini, parsnip, sweet potato, pumpkin or beetroot if you're keen to use it up.

LOVE YOUR LEFTOVERS

Look, I imagine there won't be much left when you cook these recipes but maybe you've cooked a full roast for just yourself and you're trying to figure out what to do with the leftovers. Here's some inspo . . .

Baked egg chorizo beans (page 168):
Spoon it between two slices of buttered bread, add some cheese and grill it. Baked bean toastie – yassss.

Bolognese (page 126):
Layer into a lasagne with cheat's béchamel from the crêpe recipe (page 112).

Cabbage curry noodles (page 74):
Roll up in spring roll pastry and deep fry for the tastiest spring roll ever.

Cheesy focaccia (page 96):
Turn into breadcrumbs and use in place of any recipe requiring breadcrumbs.

Crispiest pork belly (page 106):
Make a quick miso soup, add noodles and a hard-boiled egg, corn and broccoli. Slice the pork and spoon over chilli crisp and you've got yourself a quick bowl of ramen.

Deep-dish apple cobbler crumble (page 250):
Mix with store-bought ice cream, return to container and freeze to make apple cobbler ice cream.

Leggy roast chook and stuffing (page 154):
Chicken soup – throw any veg trimmings roasted chicken bones and corn cobs in a pot and cover with water. Bring to the boil and cook for 1–2 hours. Drain and add some cooked noodles, corn, spring onion, soy sauce, white pepper and chopped celery.

Pork larb (page 114):
Use to fill some crispy baked wonton wrappers for a quick canapé or toss through some noodles, broccoli and cashews for a quick stir fry.

Pulled chicken (page 236):
Roll the chicken in tortillas and transfer to a baking dish. Douse in some passata and scatter over extra spices. Cover with cheese and bake for enchiladas.

Pumped miso ginger pumpkin soup (page 46):
Serve as a puree with fish, steamed rice and veg and scatter with fresh herbs.

Slow-roasted lamb shoulder with preserved lemon (page 240):
Shred the meat and serve as soft tacos with a fresh grilled corn, tomato, coriander and lime salsa and lots of salad.

Sticky harissa glazed salmon (page 162):
Turn into a rice bowl like the tuna rice bowl on page 160.

Tandoori lamb lollypops (page 210):
Slice and use instead of chicken on the tandoori pizza on naan (page 218).

Watermelon salad (page 184):
Transfer to a blender and whiz to create a cold soup or a dressing to throw over some iceberg lettuce.

RECIPE INDEX

CONVERSION CHART

From ounces to inches, feet to fahrenheit; this is the page for you if you're in need of some imperial conversions. The good news is that tablespoon and teaspoon measures are universally covered in this book (I even factored in the Aussies), but gram weights, mls, cms and degrees will need to be converted if you're in the US and used to imperial measurements. Please be aware these are approximate only, but should convert these recipes nicely into their imperial – and delicious – doppelgänger version for you to enjoy!

DRY MEASUREMENTS

METRIC	IMPERIAL
15 g	½ oz
30 g	1 oz
60 g	2 oz
90 g	3 oz
125 g	4 oz (¼ lb)
155 g	5 oz
185 g	6 oz
220 g	7 oz
250 g	8 oz (½ lb)
315 g	10 oz
345 g	11 oz
375 g	12 oz (¾ lb)
410 g	13 oz
440 g	14 oz
470 g	15 oz
500 g	16 oz (1 lb)
750 g	24 oz
1 kg	32 oz (2 lb)

LIQUID MEASUREMENTS

METRIC	CUP	IMPERIAL
60 ml	¼ cup	2 fl oz
80 ml	⅓ cup	2¾ fl oz
100 ml		3½ fl oz
125 ml	½ cup	4 fl oz
150 ml		5 fl oz
180 ml	¾ cup	6 fl oz
200 ml		7 fl oz
250 ml	1 cup	8¾ fl oz
310 ml	1¼ cups	10½ fl oz
375 ml	1½ cups	13 fl oz
430 ml	1¾ cups	15 fl oz
475 ml		16 fl oz
500 ml	2 cups	17 fl oz
625 ml	2½ cups	21½ fl oz
750 ml	3 cups	26 fl oz
1 L	4 cups	35 fl oz

LENGTH MEASUREMENTS

METRIC	IMPERIAL
3 mm	⅛ inch
5 mm	¼ inch
1 cm	½ inch
5 cm	2 inch
10 cm	4 inch
20 cm	8 inch
25 cm	10 inch
30 cm	12 inch

OVEN TEMPERATURES

The oven temperatures in this book are for a fan-forced oven. If using a conventional oven, increase the temperature by 10-20 degrees.

CELSIUS (conventional)	CELCIUS (fan forced)	FAHRENHEIT	GAS
120°C	100°C	250°F	1
150°C	130°C	300°F	2
160°C	140°C	325°F	3
180°C	160°C	350°F	4
190°C	170°C	375°F	5
200°C	180°C	400°F	6
230°C	210°C	450°F	7
250°C	230°C	500°F	9

Where to start. First and foremost, thank you to my publisher, designer and photographer Tonia Shuttleworth. I feel very privileged to grace the Koa Press shelves and be a part of a community of local authors. Tonia absolutely nailed the design of this book and somehow channelled my personality into the pages. Working together, styling our way through all the recipes in my cosy studio in the peak of winter in freezing Christchurch, well – the memories we made will last a lifetime. Thanks for believing in this book as both a publisher and a designer: you wear both hats so effortlessly, and the success of Koa Press is a testament to that. You are an exceptionally talented human and I feel incredibly lucky to have worked with you on this project. Also thanks to Frankie (Tonia's six-year-old daughter) for patiently enjoying our after-school-care shoots and being the cutest hand model ever.

Jo Hampseed, the fluffer, the polaroid taker, the storyteller, the chopper, the washer upperer. You're an absolute legend and I'm so glad you jumped on board the COOK ME train.

Tessa King, the editor, who kept my personality on the page. Your confidence in this book and its message is incredibly empowering and motivated me to believe in myself as a first-time cookbook author. Thank you; you're exceptional.

Luke and Zoe. My people. My tiny little fam who support me without any questions. Zoe, you're currently one year old and your favourite thing to do is to play in your little kitchen and scream out 'Dada Dada Dada', which I choose to not take personally. Your infectious smile and giggles have kept me going throughout the huge task of writing my first cookbook and I'm so glad I have you by my side. Luke, you pushed me up this mountain and let me pretend I was pushing myself. Thanks for knowing exactly when to push and when to hold back. You're one heck of a partner and I love you so incredibly much.

Mum and Dad, thanks for making sure I grew up knowing what good food was and how important it was to me. I was lucky to know what I wanted to do from a really early age and you let me grab it with two hands, including letting me change schools in Year 10 to study drama, food tech, society and culture and hospitality #gamechanger.

To my family and friends, including those I roped in to do proofreads. You've been my number-one supporters and given me the confidence to put this book out into the world. Thanks for cheering me on and keeping me inspired to keep going. Love you all to bits.

To my mentors and all the awesome people I've got to work with over the years, thanks for letting me learn from you. There's so much of it in everything I do and I am eternally grateful.

I also want to extend a thank you to Akaroa Salmon, ANZCO beef and lamb and Oakley's potatoes for providing your exceptional produce for me to cook with for this book. It makes my job easy when I get to work with such high-quality ingredients.

And to you! Yes you, person reading this. You're an incredible human. Thank you for supporting someone with (currently) under 10,000 Instagram followers and who hasn't been on a reality TV show. I truly hope you cook this book, and it gets given prime pozi in your kitchen.

THANK YOU!

KOA PRESS

Published in 2022 by Koa Press Limited.
www.koapress.co.nz
@koapress

COOK ME
ISBN: 978-0-473-63522-0

10 9 8 7 6 5 4 3 2 1

Publisher and Director: Tonia Shuttleworth @koapress
Editor: Tessa King @tessaroseking_editorial
Proofreader: Anna King Shahab @radish._
Designer: Tonia Shuttleworth
Photographer: Tonia Shuttleworth
Food stylist: Sam Parish @sam.parish.food
Food assistant: Jo Hampseed
Prop stylists: Tonia Shuttleworth and Sam Parish
Copyright text © Sam Parish 2022
Copyright photography © Tonia Shuttleworth 2022
Copyright layout and design © Koa Press Limited

A catalogue record of this book is available from
the National Library of New Zealand.

Printed and bound in China by 1010 Printing.